ANCHORED

DEBORAH BAILEY

YELLOWHAMMER
PUBLISHING

Printed in the United States of America

First Printing, 2017

Print ISBN 978-0-9994938-1-6

Ebook ISBN 978-0-9994938-0-9

www.AshlynnBaileyFoundation.com

"Anchored is a riveting read that takes on one of the most volatile attacks on the family and the church. There is no family that is safe from the attack of drug addiction and Deborah Bailey takes this issue head on pulling no punches. This biblically sound devotional is a must read not only for those who are in the battle, but to also prepare for the possibility of an upcoming battle. *Anchored* sheds light on who is behind the attack and why we must be anchored to the hope found only in Christ."

— RICK BURGESS CO-HOST OF THE
RICK AND BUBBA SHOW

"For parents facing the gut-wrenching but all too common experience of walking through their children's drug addictions Deborah Bailey's "Anchored" provides the tools to wholly align their thinking on this difficult life experience with God's perspective. Seeing it God's way is practically the whole battle and "Anchored" gets you there."

Together we win,

— MARK PETTUS, HIGHLANDS
COLLEGE

Addiction never only affects the user – it always touches the family members of the addict. Anchored reminds us to not place our hope in the answers offered to us by the world but rather to tether our souls to trusting in our loving God. Deborah has provided a great source of comfort, peace and direction for heart-broken and distraught parents looking for answers and hope.

— MICAH ANDREWS, CHIEF
EXECUTIVE OFFICER-THE FOUNDRY
MINISTRIES BESSEMER, ALABAMA

"As a pastor, counselor and Christian addiction specialist, I highly recommend *Anchored* as a must read for every Christian parent who is struggling with a prodigal child mired in drugs, alcohol and other rebellious activities. Deborah has touched on every aspect of pain and healing that a parent goes through, whether married or single, while dealing with addictions in their family. This book is a great tool as study guide for support groups across America."

— ROCK HOBBS, SENIOR
PASTOR/EXECUTIVE DIRECTOR
TRANSFORMATION MINISTRIES,
BIRMINGHAM, AL

CONTENTS

INTRODUCTION

"...afraid that we were about to run aground, they threw
out four anchors and prayed for daylight."
Acts 27: 29 The Message

In Acts chapter 27, Paul and some other men were on a
ship when they encountered massive storms which had
battered their ship. One night, Paul heard from an angel
of God who said, "Do not give up." Paul knew they would
probably shipwreck somewhere, but he also believed God
would see them through to the end. Anchors signify a
major point in our lives as we battled the storm of a child
addict. But, to completely understand this point, it is
critical you know what the definition of the word
"anchor" is:

An anchor is a heavy object attached to a
rope or chain and used to moor a vessel
to the sea bottom. It can also be a
person or thing that provides stability
or confidence in an otherwise
uncertain situation.

Paul and these men did all they could physically by throwing over four anchors, and then they did what they could do spiritually; they prayed, knowing their primary Anchor was God. As storms are encountered by sailors at sea, so we will encounter storms in our lives. Some will be worse than others. When the storms first rocked our boat, I was a forty-three-year-old, happily married, Christian mother of two beautiful children. My first child, a girl, was sixteen years old. My second child, a boy, was twelve years-old. I was in an enjoyable, fulfilling, and flexible job in the medical profession. It sounds like I had a perfect life and had my act together, doesn't it? But, nothing was further from the truth. It was the calm before the storm. I could have painted a beautiful picture, because if I am a Christian, then everything in life is perfect, right? At least that is how the world thinks the Christian life should be portrayed. Unfortunately, it is how most of us pretend to act around others, especially when we are with our church family.

As a person of faith, it's hard to admit to the church, family, and friends about nasty, personal storms. I had to choose not to lie and run from the truth and life God has blessed me with so graciously. Christians are never promised a perfect life here on Earth. That is what Heaven will be like! In fact, that is how Heaven is now. However, severe, sorrow-proclaiming storms and trials will come in life here on Earth. I have had many little life storms, but this storm was one of the biggest trials of my existence. My daughter, who loved God and led others to God, was becoming a prodigal child. She was wasting away what the Lord had gifted her with.

At sixteen, she was making choices that not only affected her but everyone in her life. Her rebellion started off as regular teenage disrespect and disobedience, but the line was crossed, and the storm blew out of control in our family. It wasn't long before drugs, alcohol, and complete fits of rage entered our home. Drug addiction is a terrible storm that rips apart everyone in its path. It is a monstrosity! It rocks and batters your child and the entire family. As a parent, it may often feel you will sink and drown in the storm, but, rest assured, you are safe when you keep your eyes on the Master.

While I could write a fascinating book on our family life over the last few years, that is not what God led me to do. Through my experiences, I have found no profound solutions yet in how a parent can rescue his/her child from drug addiction. It should be noted, I have read many books, attended counseling, and have been seen by various medical professionals for my child. I have been given much advice from family and friends, I have learned a lot from the godly counsel I received, but that is not what helped me the most in this storm. The one thing that rescued me is God, His word, and my prayer time with my precious Healer, Protector, and Savior. I found my peace through anchoring myself in the Word, through prayer, and constant worship.

God "whispered" to me a little over three years ago that I should write a book about my experience to share with others going through a similar storm. In fact, I was led by God to write a book full of devotions to help other parents have scripture in their hands to help them through parenting a wayward, drug-addicted child. Prayer and knowledge of God's word are powerful battle tools. Both tools elevate authority over our troubles and raise our trust and faith in God. I let God lead me, so I have become only a vessel for His word. The emotions from my experiences during these times can be felt in these devotions. Feelings and emotions can get the best of our soul and body until we are as "strung out" as our addict child. But, through prayer and scripture, a parent can stand firm and grow in faith through the storm of addiction.

It is my desire, through these devotions, that you find peace, joy, and once again sense God's love and grace through your storm of parenting a drug-addicted child. My prayer is that you will become anchored in God's presence, His promises, and His word. I pray that you will no longer allow the raging storm of drug addiction to toss you to and fro, to the point where you cannot see God or feel His presence. And, if you do not know Jesus as your Savior, you will submit everything to Him and allow Jesus to carry you through this storm. Finally, I pray that if you are already a Christian that you will renew your trust in God and do not permit this storm to become bigger than your God.

As you begin this journey with me, I would like to share Ashlynn's story. Her story is important because it shines a light on the source of all battles with addiction. The fight is against Satan, not your child. He uses drugs and addiction as weapons of attack. Satan is our enemy and the one who seeks to steal and destroy anyone in any way to prevent God's glory and power from being revealed in this world. As you read Ashlynn's story, you can see how even though she used drugs, the Devil had already been scheming in our lives to wreak havoc to pull us away from God.

ASHLYNN'S STORY

A shlynn Nicole Bailey, born April 21, 1995, to the proud parents of Mike and Deborah Bailey. Ashlynn was a beautiful blue-eyed baby girl, tiny yet mighty. Our little girl had to stay in the step-down unit after birth because she required medical treatment for pneumonia after aspiration during the delivery process. Little Ashlynn was a fighter and strong during the healing process. She had to stay in the hospital for seven days before we could bring her home. Ashlynn was our first child and the first grandchild on both sides of our family. It wasn't long after her birth we all fell in love with her! Ashlynn had to be careful about being around people soon after her birth due to her having pneumonia; but as soon as she could attend church, we had her there. She was dedicated about eight months of age in our church's parent-baby dedication ceremony.

Growing up in church, Ashlynn learned about God and became a Christian at an early age and, in fact, it was soon after the 9/11 event that forever changed our peaceful world here in America. She loved God and had a real anointing for leading others to Christ. Ashlynn felt that everyone needed to go to Heaven and even led several of her friends to Christ.

Ashlynn loved people, adventures, having fun, and celebrating life. She was fun-spirited and never wanted to miss out on anything. Ashlynn's main struggle as a young toddler and child was handling her anger. She was usually happy, but man, when she got upset, she was upset! She was nearly impossible to console once she reached this point and would have to just calm herself down in her room alone. I mentioned this aspect because it is important later in her life story. Ashlynn loved school but had a few misfortunate events early in life that created a personal wound to her soul. She was a tiny little girl, much smaller than most children her age (but not much different from how her mom was as a baby and child). During her first few days of public kindergarten, she was ridiculed for being too short. Girls would not let her in their club because she was "too small" to be in school. She came home heartbroken, and so were her mom and dad. We parented her through this the best way we knew how. But, unfortunately, she would continue to be labeled as "short," "tiny," and "little" even throughout high school.

From the age of about seven years old, Ashlynn wanted to

be a cheerleader. She took dance lessons and gymnastics to help prepare her and began working on her cheerleading skills when she was in the sixth grade. In seventh grade, Ashlynn tried out for middle school cheerleader and made it! We remember her crying tears of joy when she found out she had made the team; she could not believe it. As parents, we thought this would help bring her the confidence she needed to overcome the low self-esteem she developed over being so little. Ashlynn continued to cheer through her sophomore year in high school and was also on a competitive cheer team as well during those middle school and high school years.

During this time, she was still kidded about being little, but she learned different coping methods to handle what she was feeling inside. She built up a tough outer exterior, but on the inside, I think it still crushed her. Ashlynn loved cheering, and you could not keep her away from practice! Once she was in high school, she decided she might even like to pursue cheering in college. An excellent, sweet, coach she had at the competitive team encouraged her with her size because most college cheerleaders need to be small as they are "flyers."

During Ashlynn's freshman year in high school, we saw noticeable changes in her behavior. Many of Ashlynn's friends changed; her grades declined from all A's to A's, B's and a C here or there and her desire to cheer and attend practice even decreased. As parents, we suspected possible drug use; but we could never find evidence. We prayed for God to reveal the truth to us, and He did in 2 ways. First, I, (her mom) awakened from a deep sleep one night to the sound of God's voice saying, "Your child is doing drugs." Second, a few days following that, she was drug-tested at school and came home upset she would fail. Initially, she told us that it was her first time of trying "weed." Later we came to find out she had been experimenting previously as well. We believe, by trying marijuana, she was only trying to fit in with her friends. Ashlynn was trying to show others she was "big enough." We think the marijuana made her feel euphoric and like she was in control. We believe it made her feel like she had no pain and no anger. That drug would just be the beginning.

As much as we tried to stay on top of things as parents with this situation, things spiraled out of control. It was simply an awful, gut-wrenching experience! She quit cheerleading by the end of her sophomore year. By then, her grades were plummeting, and she and her friends were constantly in trouble. Some of her good friends were pushing away from her; her anger and mood swings were beyond manageable; phone calls from the police and arrests were made-just one thing after another happened. She never graduated from high school because she had to be sent to a rehab the last two months of her senior year. She did well in this rehab program, came home and took the GED before attending college for a brief time. Again, the demon of drug addiction struck her again.

Through counseling sessions at the first rehab, we learned that Ashlynn had a terrible misfortune happen to her personally during high school and she could never get over it. She would use drugs to hide her pain and her self-hate. She had used most every kind of drug, but heroin was the hook line and sinker-her drug of choice. It is a tough drug to rehab from, especially in a real addict's brain. Looking back at Ashlynn's life and her personality, we believe she had addictive tendencies all along, and it took one time of the right drug for her to be ever hooked on it and the constant craving for that first experience with heroin. As we look back, we believe the devil used the drugs to devour Ashlynn because the devil knew she would be a great Christian warrior. She was a threat to him, and he went after her with a vengeance. As a family, we claimed the verse Jeremiah 29:11 over her life and our life: "For I know the plans that I have for you, declares the Lord, plans for welfare and not for calamity to give you a future and a hope." We were going to hold onto God's word no matter what the devil was throwing at us.

Over the course of several more years, Ashlynn was in and out of various rehabs. She would have brief moments of victory over her addiction. She even tried to start school again at a junior college. Ashlynn so wanted a better life for herself. She wanted to pursue a career that would help others, but the demon of addiction would eventually win out. She thought she had ruined her life forever and just could not seem to figure out how to start over. Ashlynn did not want to be an addict, and she would often state she wished she had never tried drugs. She prayed and prayed for the addiction to be taken away. She wanted to be healed instantly from the addiction! Ashlynn was under much prayer all during these tumultuous years. God was reaching out to Ashlynn in many ways, but she could not see it because she believed the devil's lies. Ashlynn eventually got into a dark place for a Christian to be in-we think she felt that her life was hopeless and that she would never be healed of the disease; we believe she felt that God had given up on her, which was what the devil wanted her to believe. It's hard to see your child in this degree of despair. I believe even as a parent of a drug addict you can get in this dark pit.

A PARENT'S JOURNEY

As a parent, each of us has hopes and dreams for our child. We want the best for them and for them to seek the best out of life. We work so hard to provide, teach, mentor and to love our child. Parenting is an incredible, exhausting full-time job. When something like drug addiction comes along, it crushes dreams, creates doubt in our parenting skills, causes us to develop feelings towards our child and those close to us we have never had before, and it will even cause us to question our faith. It causes us to question our God. Can you see how the devil is using drug addiction to not only destroy your child but to destroy you as well?

Having a child that is a drug addict will produce some crazy out-of-control emotions, thoughts, and conflicts that not only affect you personally but others as well. These emotions, thoughts, and conflicts will create an inner personal turmoil and sleeplessness.

The truth is, you won't even know who you are anymore if you let these three issues rule your life. Your relationship with your child and spouse will suffer. Your relationships with your other children, your parents, and even your friends can be negatively affected also. You will feel misunderstood, desperate, and you will pine for your old life before your child used drugs. And, while you will be willing to do most anything to stop your child from doing drugs, you can even become an enabler, which isn't what your child needs. Before long, you will isolate yourself from others, and you may even separate yourself from God; depression sets in and apathy rules because you cannot see how things will get any better. You may find yourself in a deep, dark pit and not know how to get out. If so, you have fallen for Satan's scheme, you have listened to his lies, you even believe them. Satan has you right where he wants you.

You cannot help your child, you cannot help yourself, and life has become a mess. All you need is someone to understand, someone to change everything, someone to make things right again, someone to give you peace, strength, and redemption from the pain and sorrow. Jesus is the only person who can do all of this. Somehow you must cry out to Jesus. You must lay down everything, including your child, at the foot of the cross-a complete surrender of all. Then, you must seek Him, praise Him, and worship Him, repent of allowing the storm of drug addiction to become bigger than God. Turn your focus on Jesus only. The devil created this storm, and you have quit believing and trusting God. Instead, you are trying to fix everything on your own. Jesus never left you. You were pulled astray by the devil's schemes and lies. Sometimes you must be at your lowest to want to change- just as the person addicted to drugs. Christ can resurrect us from our lowest and messiest of places.

As you read through the devotions, scriptures, and prayers, seek God with all your heart. Ask Him for His help, and you will find it. You will see your faith grow and watch God deliver you from the dark pit. You will become a well and healthy parent for your child battling addiction. Your child will notice the difference God is making in your life. Loving your child through the eyes of God may be the thing he/she needs. God's work in this storm will be a witness to others. Other people will see God's glory during the storm. You will be anchored in the midst of your storm.

PART I

BATTEN THE SHIP

In a storm, sailors will prepare the ship for the surge to come, often referred to as "batten down the ship." As the parent of a child drug addict, there are critical areas that you must "batten down." In this first section of the book, I want you to follow me on a journey of preparation for this storm of drug addiction. These are areas which must be secured from the breaches of havoc drug addiction will bring into your life.

MARRIAGE SHAKING

BECOMING ONE

"For this reason, a man will leave his
father and mother and be united to his
wife, and two will become one flesh. So
they are no longer two, but one.
Therefore, what God has joined, let
man not separate."

— MARK 10: 7-9 NIV

I am no expert in parenting, nor an expert in marriage. The words I write are a result of spending time in prayer and studying God's Word and based on the experiences I have gone through in my marriage dealing with a rebellious teen battling a drug addiction. I preface what I say with this: Marriage is complicated enough without other stresses added such as illness, disease, family, children, and careers. While all marriages should place God first, sometimes outside counseling is needed. My intentions are not to provide this book as a substitute for professional counseling, nor is my role that of a counselor. The purpose of including marriage as a topic in this book is to share the experiences I had during my marriage and to demonstrate how keeping your marriage a priority is so crucial in parenting a child addicted to drugs.

Each one of us is unique in personality, beliefs and life experiences. When a person gets married, he or she brings that uniqueness into the marriage and is expected to merge with someone with differing personality traits. Our personalities, beliefs, and life experiences affect our thoughts and actions in parenting. These differences can be a source of conflict in marriage. But woe to the marriage impacted by a rebellious teen, let alone a drug addict in the midst! You better have God front and center and the two of you better be acting and thinking like one!

My daughter developed many rebellious ways because of the drug abuse. In attempts to cover up the addiction or deny she had a problem, my daughter became an expert at the "manipulation" game. Her best game playing strategy was using one parent against the other. Sometimes she would use the expression "you always take dad's side" or "you love my brother more." When she would be told no by one parent, she would go to the other parent and try to get permission or the answer she wanted. This caused several marriage battles. Resentment was being built on all sides.

Thankfully, God did not intend our marriages to be run by our children, especially a rebellious drug addict. He intends for our marriages to founded by Him and through Him. He expects our marriages to be based on His word. The husband is the head of the household and the spiritual leader of the family. The wife is the husband's "helper" and devoted to seeking the best for her family. With God as the center of marriage, husbands and wife become one entity. They should support each other, have each other's back and love each other deeply. Children should not be placed above the sanctity of marriage. Marriage was a vow the two of you took before God. Children are a blessing from God for your marriage. When one of your children seeks to be rebellious, you must first go to God in prayer individually and then as a married couple. Decisions should only be made with God's input and based on His word. At times, you may differ in your approach. My suggestion is to let your husband be the household leader and spiritual leader. Wives you come alongside and support his decisions and help him carry them out. It is important for the rebellious child to know that he/she is loved but certain boundaries must not be crossed within your marriage. And, that the two of you work as one unit to develop your child into the person God wants him/ her to be.

Make sure that you and your husband are spending time

alone together to reconnect the love that is often stressed when raising a rebellious teen. Husbands court your wife and wives flirt with your husbands. Make each other feel special and needed. Listen to their needs. Have fun with your husband. Do not rely on your spouse to be your source of joy. Only God can be your source of joy. During stressful times, your spouse may seem distant or not there for you because he or she is dealing with his or her forms of sadness and disappointment in raising a rebellious child. Make sure you are communicating these problems with your spouse. Misunderstanding something that is said or not said can build a high wall of resentment.

A rebellious child may often have similar negative traits that your spouse possesses. It may be those little aggravating, pesky habits or attitudes that you never noticed when the two of you were dating but pop up over time. You may not have even noticed them until that rebellious child displays those attitudes. Then the child becomes the "your child did this" person instead of our child. Do not blame the spouse for any behavioral problems your child is having! That only destroys confidence in the spouse as a parent and destroys unity in the marriage. You are one now, so insulting your spouse is also insulting to you. Remember that neither your spouse nor your child is the enemy here. Seek God to correct your issues first and to provide wisdom and strength in raising your rebellious child. Be as one under God's direction. Your child even though rebellious will know that their home and family is secure. It will also show them how God works in relationships and that the marriage vow is of Him, from Him and for Him.

For those individuals that may be divorced or separated, I would still stand firm and united as parents of your child. Make every effort to put aside your differences. Seek God and respect each other out of the love and peace Christ grants to each one of us. Even though you may not be living as husband and wife, you are still parenting a child who needs the two of you to be united in the willingness to provide a source of general stability. It is crucial that the two of you find common ground on boundaries, disciplinary actions, and problem-solving efforts.

As for the single parent, where there is not a spouse involved personally with the child, I would strongly suggest having a trusted friend, mentor, and counselor that you can confide in and seek Godly advice. Parenting a child with drug addiction should never be done alone. You will need the support and counsel from others.

Dear Lord,

Thank you so much for my wonderful spouse! Thank you that he/she is such a wise and loving parent to our children. Thank you that he/she never gave up on our rebellious child and that he/she loves our child unconditionally, as You do with us. Thank you, that during trials and issues in opposing opinions, you give us peace when we ask. Forgive us for not putting You first in our thoughts and decisions. Forgive us for any resentment we have built up and replace it with respect and love. Thank you that even though our child may not have liked the "team" approach to our parenting, he/ she will see the value in our marriage. Keep our marriage safe from evil, rooted in unconditional love, growing in you. Make us wise and loving parents to our child. Grant us peace during trials that may come. Strengthen our unity, so our power in You increases.

-Amen

QUESTIONS FOR THOUGHT:

- Are my spouse and I acting in one accord in our parenting of our addict child?
- Do my spouse and I communicate regularly (in a respectful, peaceful manner) the daily issues that arise with our wayward child? And with our discussion, are we problem solving to meet the needs of our child and not own agendas?
- Do my spouse and I pray together about our marriage; our children? Do we seek God first in all we do as a married couple and as a parent of a drug addict child?
- Am I putting my child and this drug issue before my marriage? Am I neglecting the one I made a

vow with "for better or for worse"? What efforts am I making to spend time reconnecting with my spouse as a married couple?

- Am I, as a wife, trying to rule over my husband and take his place as the spiritual leader in our home? Am I nagging and complaining to him, or am I seeking ways to be his helper gracefully and lovingly helping with the issues at hand? Am I, as a husband, trying to dictate my home under my own rules, or am I seeking God's will and wisdom in leading my home? Do I love my wife as Christ loves the church-am I nurturing and protecting her?

BOUNDARIES

"You're blessed when you stay on course,
walking steadily on the road revealed
by God."

— PSALM 119:1 THE MESSAGE

I love these verses, especially The Message Bible translation. Directions for following boundaries are easily explained in these verses. This message from God, through David, is an excellent source for my children and each of us as parents. As a mother, I want my children to obey me like this scripture details. I can only imagine how easy life would be if my children walked the way I told them, followed my directions, and then, thanked me for showing them the way. I would never have to discipline my children. That would be a wonderful life, but, it rarely works out this way in parenting!

I believe we are blessed with freedom when we follow God's way and not our own way. When we walk the walk, no matter what our child does or how our child acts, we are demonstrating exactly what God expects. However, we often made the mistake of seeking our way instead of asking for God's direction. When we seek our own way, in parenting, marriage, or anything in life, it separates us from the fullness God has for us. In my own situation, I was the one that went off course. Once I realized the pit I had fallen in, I cried out to the Lord for help. God graciously rescued me and redirected my steps as a parent. My circumstances did not change, but I was choosing to be obedient to God's direction, and that makes a world of difference.

My family life runs much more smoothly when each one of us is trying to walk in God's ways. When we stood by the principles of God's word, we encountered opposition with our drug-addict child. Now, it wasn't that my daughter was knowingly opposing God, but she was opposed to "the rules" we set as parents, the rules we adopted through God's word. These are the same principles God gives us as His children- not to torment us and hold us prisoner, but they are His guidelines He designates because He loves us and wants no harm to bestow us. As we grow closer to God, we want to obey His commands. Consequently, as we obey God, we are expressing love towards Him. My child, however, could not see that full obedience to God leads to blessings and freedom. She still, even though she was a child of God, meandered off on her path much like David and very much like Israel.

The drug addict wants his/her way because of an overwhelming bodily desire to satisfy the craving of their drug of choice. A drug addict's brain is truly not capable of making a rational decision. Right and wrong become clouded-they are in survival mode-running on animal instinct to get what they need at all costs. The drug addict is willing to go against their own family, authority and God's ways to satisfy the drug craving.

As a parent of an addict, the opposition and the relentless torture of watching the depravity of your child seeking drugs begin to wear on you mentally and emotionally. You are willing to do anything to make the craziness stop. I began to question if standing up to God's ways was helping my daughter. I even began to relax boundaries I thought I would never cross in my household just to have a little peace. But, I did not get the peace-instead more violent turmoil was a result. I decided to go off on my own to seek my own peace, and that is when things spiraled out of control. I had to get back on the path that God designed me to follow if I was ever going to be able to help my daughter.

God does not change His laws to meet the needs of His

people, especially when they get off course. Instead, He changes the people to become more like Him through a series of painful events. The painful events were not created by God. They are caused by the choices we make in pathways. Our choices and the resulting consequences cause the pain. God uses those results as a discipline tool. We must lean heavily on Him to get us through our consequences as we change direction and get back on the right path.

As a mother, I came to a sobering realization: I cannot change my daughter, and, my husband cannot change my daughter. But, as a couple, as parents, we resolved to not change our God-directed household rules. We have boundaries set in place to protect our family and home. Here's what these boundaries do for our family:

These boundaries were formed out of love and to keep harm from each one in our family. These limits do not include the use of drugs within our household. A set of guidelines have been instated in which certain due consequences and penalties are enacted. Forgiveness, grace, and truth are ever present in the midst. A definitive boundary has been drawn in the home: Continued drug use without seeking any means of help will result in being removed from the family environment. As a minor, our child had the only choice of drug rehabilitation. As she became an adult, she had two options of which she could make-one was drug rehabilitation, the other option was her living outside our home independently. These boundaries may sound cruel and inhumane, but it is a form of intervention to bring the drug addict to his/her senses.

In the Bible, the parable of the prodigal child is similar. Just as the father in the parable of the prodigal child let his son leave, God will allow us out on our own, but He never leaves us. He is always right there waiting for our return home. We are free to choose to follow our own desires, but, if we want to go against His ways, God will let us meander in the desert. He will implement any form of consequence to bring us back to Him because He loves us too much to leave us in our own misery. As a parent, I am not abandoning my drug addict child. I have set before my child specific boundaries which have a consequence if crossed. It is my child that is making a choice. I will never leave my child. I am always right here for my child to support and assist her willingness to be drug-free. I am not here to allow her to continue to use the drugs. I must rely on God's strength to keep these boundaries. As my child continues to go her own way, I place my faith in God that as my child seeks Him, He will transform her into the person He designed her to be. My prayer is she will choose His path and not continue down the wrong path.

God is a God of order. Boundaries were given by God in the very beginning in the Garden of Eden because He knows our tendency to stray. We are only blessed with freedom, peace, joy, and fullness of life when we choose to walk in God's direction, stand up for God's laws, and live within God's loving boundaries. When we love God as He meant us to love Him, we will be obedient, and it will be easier to make the right choice.

Dear Lord,

Thank you that you have a right path for us to follow, one that leads to freedom, peace, and closer to You. Thank you for not letting us stay lost in our way. Thank you for directing us back where we must go. Thank you for the challenging situations and pain that we must endure to realize that we are way off track. Thank you for the grace You give us. Thank you for being by our side-a compass for us to follow. Give us strength and grace to stand for Your ways, Lord, as we parent our wayward child. Grant us wisdom as we develop boundaries of grace and truth in our home. Give us the strength to protect our boundaries when they are crossed. Give us peace, that as we intervene with consequences for boundaries crossed, Lord, that you will never leave us, nor our child; but that You are always there awaiting our return home.

Amen

Additional Scripture References:

*You are blessed when you follow his
directions, doing your best to find him.
That's right-you don't go off on your*

*own; you walk straight along the road
he set. You, God, prescribed the right
way to live; now you expect us to live
it. Oh, that my steps might be steady,
keeping to the course you set; Then I'd
never have any regrets in comparing
my life with your counsel. I thank you
for speaking straight from your heart; I
learn the pattern of your righteous
ways. I'm going to do what you tell me
to do; don't ever walk off and leave me.*

— PSALM 119:1-8 THE MESSAGE

QUESTIONS FOR THOUGHT:

- Have my spouse and I established boundaries within our home that are in line with God's will and God's guidelines?
- Am I as a parent, following God's boundaries or am I off on my own, meandering the desert?
- Do each of my children, including my wayward child, understand the importance of these boundaries? Do each of our children know that the boundaries are established with truth and grace and designed out of love to protect and nurture? Do each of my children know the consequences of crossing the boundaries?

LACK OF TRUST

"Far better to take refuge in God than to trust people;"

— PSALM 118:8 THE MESSAGE

Trust can be defined as the reliance on the integrity, strength, and ability of a person or thing. Trust is developed with people based on the time we spend with them and in direct relationship to how those people respond towards us when we need them to have integrity; when we need them to be strong for us; when we need an able body to be there. In modern terms, trust is "having someone's back" and not compromising that relationship out of selfish ambition or needs.

As parents, we never trust our newborns. We don't know

what to expect from them. They trust us for everything even without knowing us for long. They cannot survive without what we can provide for them. Once our babies have reached a few months of age, they seem to know us as their family. They, in turn, act differently towards strangers. Some have called it separation anxiety. I wonder, however, if maybe our babies trust us as parents because of the time we have spent with them to meet their needs, to be true, and to be dependable for them, whereas a stranger has not yet developed that trusting relationship with them.

As our children grow, parents start to trust them as individuals. As parents, our trust is mainly in the form of integrity. Is that child going to act the way he or she should even when we are not there directly supervising them? Most children will test us in the areas of trust. We as humans just want our way and sometimes make bad choices. As our children make wise decisions and obey us as parents, we begin to entrust them with more responsibilities and activities. Once a child deviates from obedience and makes a poor decision, our trust of that child erodes. As parents, we usually discipline the child's erroneous behavior or action; and with time, we start to build that trust relationship again, if that child continues to obey us and continues to develop that integrity characteristic when we are not standing over them.

It is a challenge to trust a wayward, rebellious child, a child in bondage to drugs. Without trust, any relationship will deteriorate. That child even though may behave wrong, still needs us to trust them or believe in them for some reason. And as parents, we need to be able to trust our child. The lack of trusting my child has created an anxiety; a fear of the unknown, and a sense of failure in my parenting skills. These feelings are from the devil to steal my joy and hope that Christ has promised me and has given to me.

All parents go through that trust building process with any child. I must address the uniqueness of the situation though with a wayward child, especially with an addict. A wayward child wants his or her way no matter what. Their own needs and desires are more important than anything else. You may have experienced a child who will say and do anything to survive and to fulfill their drug need. An addict child will become an expert liar and a creative manipulator. They have a keen sense of what makes you tick; what gets under your skin; and what opens your emotional heart-to make you believe them. With our daughter, there came a time when we could not even begin to understand what the truth was anymore. We so wanted to believe her when she would say she wanted to be done with the drugs and her lifestyle. When she would cry, and beg for our help when she was in trouble or withdrawing, we knew "this is it, she will finally change." For moments or even for months her actions would begin to build our trust again. Only to be defeated by the bondage of drugs and rebellious ways. It truly was an ugly place and a horrible relationship to be in with your child. I truly wondered how I would ever trust my child and have a normal parent-child relationship again. Then, God's still small voice spoke to my heart. I was never to trust in man. I was only to trust in God! What an answer in the midst of painful situation! Until my daughter trusts in God and not trust in mind altering drugs, I don't have to trust her. She is living out of the flesh. She is fulfilling her selfish human desires just like each one of us does when we begin to trust ourselves and men more than we are confident in God.

Only God can restore our relationships with our wayward children. We can only trust Him with such a monumental task. While I may be tempted to fix my child, I am only required to trust God will deliver my child from the bondage of drugs and rebellion. Even in the most difficult of situations, when I can do nothing else, I can trust that God will make good of all things for those who love Him and serve His calling according to His will. I can only trust that He has this situation, and that He is bigger than the problem of rebellion and drugs. He is greater than the problem of a shattered relationship with my daughter right now. For me, it was important to remember when I felt powerless, I can only trust that God has a plan for me, a plan that is healthy and not harmful to me. Each of us, in our weakest moments, can trust that God is the Healer of all diseases including addiction and spiritual rebellion. We can trust God has conquered evil and it will not succeed forever. We should trust and believe God's ways are higher than our ways. Man will inevitably fail me because he is man and not God.

Remember this: Trust God that the grief and anxiety created by failed trust between our children and us will be replaced with the Peace of God. I also know that it is okay if I don't trust my child because my trust is to be placed in my Lord. He will never fail me, and He will never leave me. He will restore all things in His timing on Earth and Heaven.

Dear Lord,

Forgive my lack of trust in You when things get complicated and painful. Forgive me for placing other relationships above my relationship with you. Please replace the pain of the broken relationship I have with my child right now with Your peace and love. Thank you for continuing Your work in me and Your work in my child to set things right between us. Deliver us from the evil placed before our family. Thank you for being all-knowing and all-powerful in your ways. Thank you for being a God I can trust, believe, and place my hope in. It is the only way I can make it through this dark time in my life. I will put my trust in You, God, and seek You as my refuge.

Amen.

QUESTIONS FOR THOUGHT:

- Even though I may not trust my drug-addict child, do I show my child no matter what she/he can trust me?
- Do I trust God? Am I able to have peace that He knows what is best for me and that He has a plan for me?
- Am I going to God with my deepest needs and desires? Am I sincere and open with Him? Am I searching in His Word to know Him better? Am I studying and realizing how much God truly loves and cares for me? And the lost?

ADVICE FROM OTHERS

*"Take good council and accept correction-
that's the way to live wisely and well.
We humans keep brainstorming
options and plans, but God's purpose
prevails."*

— PROVERBS 19:20-21 THE
MESSAGE

As a parent, I tried my best to raise my children
to be people of good character. As a Christian
parent, I also worked to instill in my children
the ways of the Lord; and, I strived to do my best to lead
my children to the Lord. I followed advice from my
parents, from child rearing books, from my church and
the Bible.

Then, I began to discover my perfect world was unraveling. I began to realize my child was straying. I realized my daughter was become increasingly rebellious. The morals and principles I worked so hard to instill in my child were becoming obsolete. I hardly recognized my child. Not only had the child's outward appearance changed, but the inward appearance is nothing like it should be. I ultimately discovered that my child was doing drugs. And within a few short years, my daughter had become a full-blown addict.

My mind was filled with questions. And, as a parent, I knew I needed to guide my child out of this evil dark place she was headed in. Through these trying years, I have often been at a loss of what to do. Do I send her to rehab? Where is the best rehab? Do I let her stay in jail, give her another chance, trust her, or do I kick her out? On the outside, the answers to these questions may seem obvious. But, as a parent, the love I feel for my child and the need to protect that child is overwhelming. There were times I felt blind to knowing what to do.

Let me say, my husband and I sought a lot of advice from wise counsel: Godly parents; friends; counselors; pastors; and doctors. It was just confusing! There were times we ignored some excellent advice, and on the flip side, we followed some terrible advice sometimes. Ultimately, it took also seeking the Lord with all our might to find the answers to know what advice to follow. Looking back, even when we followed bad advice or ignored good advice, God worked it out according to His plan. It took a little longer going our route when we did not follow God's lead. But, He has been with us all along.

Being an experienced parent of an addict, I would suggest seeking advice from those who are knowledgeable about addiction. It is especially wise to seek counsel from those who are not only experts about addiction but Christian as well. There are so many variables and factors to consider in the mind, body, and spirit of an addict. A person who knows nothing of addiction cannot fathom all the chemical, physical and emotional things that are going on within the addict. Their advice, though well-meant, is usually an opinion rather than good counsel.

Combining the expert on addiction with strong Christian faith is just the icing on the cake. A Christian counselor should know that as humans we are a body, soul, and spirit. All three aspects of people are compromised by drug addiction. Their wisdom of both addiction and that of Christ can provide some steps for you to follow.

Being in a support group with other believers who have had similar situations lends help and wise counsel as well. It allowed me to learn about myself and others in similar circumstances. It let me know that I am not alone. I learned to let go of things I could not control and give it to God. It also allowed me to build someone else up that was as broken as me. That brought me joy in the midst of adverse circumstances.

Along with seeking counsel and support, you should be in constant prayer and study of His Word to find the wisdom only God can give. The Lord will provide you with the answer. You will know it is the right answer because it will align with His word and His ways. A sense of peace will be present, and confusion will be gone. Some of the decisions will be very difficult if not impossible to follow as a parent, but if it is what God is leading you to do, you must not go in any other direction!

Dear Lord,

Please give me the wisdom to make the right decisions. Lead me to wise counsel. Provide me with your strength to follow through with the path you lead us to. Thank you for fixing what I may have messed up, for guiding me as a parent as I struggle with my child, listening to my constant prayer; Thank you for your Word to guide me. Allow me to be still, to block out the world's noise and hear You.

Amen

QUESTIONS FOR THOUGHT:

- Am I as a parent, listening to all the advice being thrown my way or am I choosing Godly counsel?
- Do the persons I am seeking advice from have

both a clear understanding of addiction and a follower of Christ?

- Am I confused with the advice? Do I need to fervently seek God through prayer and reading His word? Do I need to be still and block the noise of others to hear the voice of my God?

GIVING YOUR CHILD TO GOD

*"I have prayed for this child, and God gave
me what I asked for. And now I have
dedicated him to God. He's dedicated
to God for life"*

— 1 SAMUEL 26 THE MESSAGE

I love the verse from 1 Samuel 26. It is an acknowledgment that my child's life is precious and a gift from God. It is a promise that as a parent, I will do everything I can to teach my child about God and to raise my child in Christian environment. The scripture prayer above was a vow from Hannah to God for blessing her with Samuel. It shows the fulfillment of that promise and reveals God's plan for Samuel to be a Levite priest. I think it is a perfect verse for parents to use as a personal praise to God for their child and a great reminder of our Christian responsibilities as parents in raising our children as God expects.

This verse does not mean that my child will become a priest, or that my child can be saved by this verse. This verse means that my child is a gift from God and that God loves my child way more than I do. God designed my child exactly as He thought best. It is my responsibility to raise my child in God's ways to the best of my abilities. God has given me a blessing, and, I, in turn, make sure my child knows who God is and devote my child to God.

Proverbs 22:6 also relates to this scripture in 1 Samuel. I am to acknowledge my responsibility as a parent so that one day as my child grows and matures, he will cling to and grasp that which is from God. It does not mean my child will be perfect. God knows that mistakes will be made, but if I have been obedient to God and trained my child in His ways, then, all I can do as the child becomes an adult is to trust God with my child. I must place my child in His good hands.

When my daughter was born, she had to stay in the step-down unit for newborns for about a week for unexpected, but common delivery issues. She was a fighter from the get go and so independent even as a tiny baby. God had given her a strong spirit. We had to wait several months before she could take part in the parent-child dedication at our church due to her hospitalization at birth. It was important to us that she was raised in Church. We took our child to church almost every Sunday. If we missed, it was because of being on vacation or illness. She took part in vacation bible school each summer. She went to a Christian preschool. We as parents taught her about God as much as possible.

Our daughter became a Christian at an early age. As a child, my daughter was comfortable talking about God to others; and she was genuinely concerned about the salvation of others. My child during her adolescent and pre-teen years led several of her friends to Christ.

It was during her teenage years that she strayed from God. She began to change friends and change interests. Looking back at what I know now, those changes probably occurred because of low self-esteem my daughter felt for herself because of being ridiculed for being "so short" as others often mocked her at school. That sweet spirit that she had as a child became a hardened tough shield as a teenager. She was tough as nails on the outside. She pretended to be unable to be hurt on the inside.

Parenting became difficult because of this tough girl rebellion. We made mistakes in our parenting during these difficult years. Our mistakes were not meant to hurt our daughter. We thought we were being Godly parents and doing the right thing. But the self-hate she had for herself along with our unintentional mistakes in parenting, only pushed her to be more rebellious and seek forms of behavior and things to soothe and ease her pain.

Before long, our daughter had become influenced by the demon of drugs and other self-destructive behaviors. Deep down she knew that what she was doing was not right in the eyes of God; and, the devil used that to convince her mind that she had gone too far for God to forgive her. This just caused more pain and self-hatred for my daughter.

We were at wit's end with what to do as parents. My husband and I were on our knees every hour of the day praying for what to do. God made it obvious that we had no control. Our family life was out of control. He made it clear we had to give our daughter back to Him completely and give Him complete control of our daughter's life. I guess we were doing what we thought was best as parents, but we were still not allowing God to be the focus in the midst of our troubles.

We were trying to hold on to control of our problems- "handle it ourselves" because we were the parents. But my daughter needed outside help that only God could provide. As we gave God control, we saw God working for the good in our lives. Our burden was lifted, and we could hear more clearly from God. God pointed us directly to send our daughter to a Teen Challenge program five states away. This was the hardest thing I have ever had to do in my life so far, but the way God had provided.

This verse from 1 Samuel spoke volumes to me as we sent her off to rehab five states away. I had prayed, like Hannah, for my baby before she was born. God graciously blessed me with my daughter. My husband and I dedicated her to the Lord and sought responsibility to raise her in God's ways. She became a Christian at an early age. God had her as His child then, and He has her now.

I had to remember that! I had to keep in mind that she was His child forever and He was dedicated forever to hold onto His sheep and to run after His sheep when it became lost. We had to give her back to Him. I had to claim Proverbs 22:6 as a prayer for her as well. I had to lay aside any doubt of myself as a parent and remember the good things I taught her. I had to hold on to the hope that one day she would return to God and us.

Dear Lord,

Thank you for my child. Thank you for being dedicated forever to my child and my child to you through Your saving grace! Help me always keep You first in rearing my child, committing all my parenting ways to Your ways. Thank you for being my Heavenly Father and saving me! I am a child of God! My child is a child of God!

Amen

ADDITIONAL SCRIPTURE REFERENCES:

"Train a child in the way he should go, and when he is old, he will not turn from it," (Proverbs 22:6 NIV).

QUESTION FOR THOUGHT:

If I have been obedient to God and taken responsibility to devote my child to God; if I have acknowledged that my child is a gift from God why am I not trusting God more with my child? Why am I holding on to my child as if I am the only one that knows the answers?

CONSTANT PRAYER

"Pray at all times."

— 1 THESSALONIANS 5:17 THE
MESSAGE

Prayer is open communication with God. It is a time to thank God; a time to worship God; a time to repent and be forgiven by God; a time to let God know our thoughts, wants, and needs. As I grow closer to God, I have come to realize that everything needs to be done in prayer. If I act on my own without praying, I often make the wrong decisions. I have also learned to pray not only when problems arise, but to pray when things are going smoothly. There have been times when things were going well that my communication with God was at its worst. Then, when the storm came, I was at a loss-what to do; who to talk to; who to help me. If I had been in constant communication with the Lord, I would not have experienced such sheer panic.

When we have children, we are more aware of the need of prayer than ever before. Those babies did not come with an instruction manual! Having a wayward child makes you fall to your knees! It took going through the painful experiences with my daughter for me to learn the importance of constant prayer. I wish I had developed a consistent prayer life before I got married and before I had children. I depended on my communication with my husband and my children to meet my emotional need. What I needed was constant communication with Jesus through prayer to meet my spiritual needs. Then, I would have been prepared to handle life at home more effectively.

Because I was not used to being in constant prayer and praying always, when my daughter began to revolt, I honestly did not know how to pray for her. I just wanted her fixed and fixed now! I was a demanding child of God. I also seemed to be praying with little faith. Just saying the same prayer to God for him to do something to stop my daughter from acting the way she was repeatedly.

I believe there is a verse in the Bible about that kind of praying. God says those doubting prayers are like waves being blown by the wind-adrift at sea (James 1:7). Consequently, the verses preceding say, *"If you don't know what you're doing, pray to the Father. He loves to help. You'll get his help, and won't be condescended to when you ask for it. Ask boldly, believingly, without a second thought"* (James 1:5-6 The Message).

God heard my prayer, but I lacked faith. I believe God wanted me to mature my faith and my prayer life. As I read His Word, I saw how little faith I had. I had to believe that one day He would answer my prayer. Throughout the past few years, God has answered many of our prayers about our daughter. She is not 100% where she should be, but I know God is working both with her and our family to mature us into the Christians we are meant to be.

A believing prayer leads to peace and gives you a sense of direction that God wants you to follow while He is working out His plan for our lives. It may not be an immediate answer, but you know it is coming! It is coming in His perfect timing! So, in the meantime, I will keep praying without any doubts. I will pray without ceasing, knowing that He is going to answer my prayer because He wants everyone to come to Him, and He goes after those who are lost!

When the storm comes, I will hold onto my Anchor and not let the waves toss me around with the wind for I know He is there.

Dear Lord,

Thank you for teaching me how to pray boldly, constantly, and without doubt! Hold me tight as I go through the storms with my child for in the end, I know that You will settle us on solid ground.

Amen

QUESTIONS FOR THOUGHT:

- Am I praying for my drug addict child consistently and with persistence? Or have I given up?
- Am I praying boldly and without doubt? Or am I doubting and just being tossed like a ship on a stormy sea?
- Am I asking God how to pray for my child?
- In my prayer, am I asking God to reveal my heart and make any changes in me that need to be made?
- After I have prayed and say Amen (which means "so be it"), do I acknowledge that God has heard my prayer and that He will answer my prayer in His perfect timing and in His way?

LOVE

"Love never gives up. Love cares more for others than for self. Love doesn't want what it doesn't have.

— 1 CORINTHIANS 13: 4-8 THE MESSAGE

This verse describes how God loves me! I never knew how much God loved me until I had my own children, and I felt that unconditional love for each of my children. There is nothing my children could do to change my love for them, and that is the type of love the Father has for each of us. I love the way my children look, their personalities, the sounds of their laughs, the way they love, everything about them. I love each of my children's soul and the spirit that God has placed in them. However, there are times, as a parent, I dislike my child. Not that I don't like the child for who he/she is though; it is that I don't like the way the child is acting or behaving.

"To you who are ready for the truth, I say this. Love your enemies. Let them bring out the best in you, not the worst. When someone gives you a hard time, respond with the energies of prayer for that person.
Luke 6:27-28 (The Message)

With a rebellious child, sometimes stress and frustration cloud the unconditional love that I should have for my child. My daughter was a rebellious teen. She was hell bent on having her own way no matter what the cost or what the consequences of her behavior may bring. Some of her rebellious ways went against my moral compass and against God's ways. No matter how much we punished her for her blatant disobedience, she would often repeat the same rebellious act or display the same rebellious attitude.

Because of her drug use, it allowed the Devil to have a stronghold in her life. Her behavior, her thoughts, her actions, and her choices were most often led by her flesh-filled desires and wants; and they were controlled by the devil's trickery and lies instead of God's truths. The drugs have control over her personality and behavior. During these tumultuous times with my daughter, I had times when I disliked her. Sometimes, I could not stand to be in the same room with her and, at times, I even dreaded to see her. Then, it hit me like a ton of bricks. Wow! Is this the way God feels about me when I go against His ways when I sin repeatedly? My dislike of her behavior and choices has brought out the worst in me.

We all fall short. Each one of us wants our own way. We are rebellious children in God's eyes; yet, He loved us enough that He sent His perfect Son, who never rebelled against His Father, to die for us on a cross, the punishment we each deserve for our selfish, sinful ways. God loves all mankind. He loves the sinner, and He loves the saint. I believe that when a person sins, it causes grief and pain to the heart of God. Sin creates a divide between the person and God. Through our acceptance of Christ as our Savior, God can stand to be in the same room with us when we sin; and He always wants to spend time with us. He expresses His love to us the way 1 Corinthians 13:4-8 describes love, because God's character is love, He *is* love.

My husband gave me a card with these verses on it when we got engaged. We have tried to base our marriage on these verses. Little did I know that these same verses are excellent guidelines for the parental love of a rebellious child. God had to spell this kind of love out for us as humans because He is the only one that can love perfectly and purely in this way. We are all God's children, each of us, even in our rebellion. God loves each of us no matter what! We, in turn, can love our wayward child just as God loves us. As a challenge, place your name anywhere the word love is in these verses. It is a good reality check. Are you full of God's love?

As a parent of a drug addicted child, I have not even come close to loving my child how God loves me; but, that does not mean that I should not strive every day to love my child in the same way. Love is a choice. It is an action, not a feeling. I choose to love no matter what a person is doing or how a person is behaving. I must love God more and more each day. I must accept God's love for me each day. I must ask God to fill me with overflowing love for others... then, the choice to love is natural, and the actions of love are fulfilled.

I also must remember that because of the drug addiction, my child is living in the flesh, and the devil has a stronghold over her. It is not my child that I dislike. Rather, it is the Devil who is my enemy, not my daughter. Luke 6:27-28 has taught me that my job right now is to love my human enemy but despise the Devil. I am to pray for my daughter, and in the name of Jesus rebuke the Devil from her life and our life. All of which needs a Holy Father to perform, and a mature, yet childlike faith from me. I am still learning this one, but the more I lean on Christ, pray without ceasing, keep my thoughts and heart pure, and guard my tongue, the easier it is to have faith for what I cannot see or control, and to fight the Devil! I cannot have any doubts whatsoever! I must ask the Lord to fill me with His love and grace so that it overflows from me to my daughter. I must love her through the eyes and heart of Christ. No matter her choices and actions, I must allow God to bring out the best in me and not display my worst towards her. Otherwise, how else will my daughter truly know the love of Christ?

Dear Lord,

Thank You that You are love! Please forgive my inadequate love for others and my child. Thank You for reminding me that I am just as rebellious as my child is. Forgive me that I want my way all the time. Forgive my rebellious nature. Thank you, Lord, for helping me realize it is not my child that I dislike. It is the Devil who is seeking to destroy my family and weaken our faith. Thank You that You are the ultimate Victor! When times get difficult, remind me who my true enemy is and help me respond with prayer over my child. I am more than a conqueror through Christ Jesus who strengthens me. Lord, Jesus, fill me with your abundant love and grace so that it overflows towards others no matter how others may act or behave towards me. I love You, Lord and I accept that You love me no matter what. Please fill me with Your love overflowing that I may love unconditionally as You do.

Amen

ADDITIONAL SCRIPTURE REFERENCES:

> *"Love doesn't strut, doesn't have a swelled head, doesn't force itself on others, isn't always "me first", doesn't fly off the handle, doesn't keep score of the sins of others, doesn't revel when others grovel, takes pleasure in the flowering of truth, puts up with anything, trusts God always, always looks for the best, never looks back, but keeps going to the end."*

— I CORINTHIANS 13:4-8

QUESTIONS FOR THOUGHT:

- Do I truly know how much God loves me?
- Am I basing my love for God, my child, and myself on feelings and emotions; or am I basing my love from God's perspective-unconditionally and through choice and obedient action?
- Do I recognize who the true enemy is in this battle with addiction?
- Are my child's behavior and choices bringing out the best in me or the worst in me?
- While I hate the evil of drugs and I as a parent

will take a stand against this evil, is my child seeing that my love for him/her will never give up and that my love for my child is unconditional? Or am I showing love through my feelings-judgment, selfishness; anger; impatience; unforgiveness?

PART II

THROWING IN THE ANCHOR

You have prepared your ship against the wind, waves, and rain that come with a child bound by addiction by becoming as one in your marriage; by trusting only God, seeking wise counsel, giving your child to God, by praying without ceasing, and by learning to love unconditionally. Now you are ready to throw in the anchor. With the release of the anchor, you are letting go of some baggage you are carrying and ridding yourself of the lies of the enemy so that once the anchor has reached its Rock, you shall not be moved as you battle the storm of addiction with your child.

ANGER

*"In your anger, do not sin. Do not let the
sun go down while you are still angry,
and do not give the devil a foothold."*

— EPHESIANS 4:26-27 NIV

Anger is a tremendous emotion often expelled with a rebellious child; unless you are a saint. I used to think being angry was a sin. Though rarely, anger is an emotion that God expresses in the Bible. Jesus even knew this emotion. I am made in His image, so anger is an emotion that I feel as well. If you are angry, this is not a sin. The key is just not to sin in our anger, to get over it, and forgive those who made us angry.

As a parent with my wayward child, I did not handle the

emotion of anger well. To be candid, I sinned numerous times in my anger. It usually takes me awhile to get angry, unless I am tired or stressed. A child addicted to drugs will make you tired and stressed; so, over the last few years, I became angry often. At times, I was so angry at my child, I not only thought bad things, but they came out of my mouth! Thankfully, God convicted me of my sin, and I sought forgiveness from Him and from my child. Notice God did not condemn me. Unfortunately, some of those times took several days for me to ask forgiveness because I thought I was justified in my anger. I mean who wouldn't be angry and have a raging fit when your drug addict child repeatedly disobeys, blatantly disrespects you by screaming profanities at you and other family members, or even shows violent behavior towards you or your property.

My husband and I disciplined our child for exhibiting those behaviors. Our daughter was often grounded, stripped of her cell phone, lost driving privileges, and, sometimes, everything was taken away. The punishment was justified, and an expected duty as a parent. But my own fits of rage that resulted in using profanity or name calling of my child was not justified! I was sinning in my anger. I gave the devil a foothold and was being myself a rebellious child of God.

To be even more candid, I let my anger build up as resentment towards my child. I did nothing to deserve this upheaval that was occurring in my household. So, I let my anger fester. At one point, my anger had taken such control over me, I would resent people who seemed to have perfect children. In fact, I would get angry at people trying to give advice, because how could they understand what I was going through. I would also get mad at my other child for no good reason just because I let that anger manifest itself into sin. I even got angry with God at times and would go for days without praying or reading my daily devotions. Sometimes I did not even go to church. What a foothold I had given to the devil.

As a family, we went to counseling for reasons related to her drug use. During counseling, we learned how to manage all the anger that was being expressed. But, it took God getting my attention and convicting me of my sin. Graciously He did not pour out His wrath on me like I deserved. He forgave me of my sin of mishandling my anger. I asked for forgiveness from my child for sinning in my anger, and I forgave my child for what was making me angry. I am still not perfect nor where I hope to be one day with dealing with anger, but I am trying to be more slow to anger. I must read my Bible often to hear what God has to say about anger. God revealed that I was never meant to harbor anger. I needed to give it to Him. He had to show me who I was fighting against.

One of my favorite verses about anger comes from Ephesians 4:26-27. This is one to follow precisely because sinning in anger has consequences which are very painful. Letting anger manifest into sin is like cancer to the soul. It is best to let your child know you are angry and why you are angry. Speak truth over the situation. Show grace just as Christ does with us. There may be just cause to discipline the child or consequences warranted if the child has does something wrong-but remember your goal is to teach and guide to promote better behavior-not punish out of anger. Settle the cause of the anger and let the anger go before you sleep because the devil will have a foothold. Not that anger about a wayward child is bad-it is not ours to hold on to because it will manifest into sin. Our anger is real, but God must be the one to take that emotion and be the One who manages this emotion in our life-not us! Ask God to replace your anger with peace and love that only He can do when you are angry.

Dear Lord,

Thank you that it is okay to be angry. But Lord, please do not let me sin in my anger. Please fill me with love and compassion towards my child, even when I am angry. Help me be slow to anger. Help me give my anger to You and forgive quickly before the sun goes down. Keep the Devil away when anger is felt. Give us Your wisdom in dealing with our anger towards our own child. Help me speak truth with grace.

Amen

QUESTIONS FOR THOUGHT:

- Do I sin against my child and others because of anger about my child and his/her drug use?
- Does God lash out His anger on me or does He speak truth with grace, convict but not condemn to promote repentance or turning from my sin? Do I show the same Godly anger towards my child?
- Do I release my anger to God and allow healing and peace within my soul so that the devil does not have a foothold on me? Or do I choose to hang on to my anger, let it fester, allow bitterness and rage to consume me so that I am not only sinning against others but against God?
- Once I lay down my anger and give it to God, do I ask God to fill me with His peace and wisdom?

GUILT

"Guilt is banished through love and truth;
Fear-of-God deflects evil."

— PROVERBS 16:6 THE
MESSAGE

A s a mother of a wayward child, I am guilty of sinning as a parent; and I have known guilt even after I confessed my sin to God and knowing He forgave my sin. If you ever dealt with a child who has done something for the 100th time, you know the emotion of total rage and frustration. Maybe you degraded your child as a person, or made them feel making things right again would cost them, or even neglected to discipline your child out of pure exhaustion. This is the reality of parenting a child addicted to drugs. I am guilty of sinning as a parent and I have even felt that it is my fault that my daughter behaves as she does and uses drugs because of my failures as a parent.

Thankfully, Christ died for my sin and when I cry out for forgiveness My God forgives me. It says in Proverbs 16:6 that guilt is removed through love and truth. God is love, and God is truth. When we accept Jesus as our Savior, confess our sin and seek forgiveness our transgressions are removed and our relationship with Him is restored. Hence, we are no longer guilty. We may experience some consequences to deal with and earthly relationships to repair, but God has wiped the slate clean.

So, if God has forgiven my sins in parenting and I am given a fresh start why do I sense so much guilt? I feel guilty for even trying to write this devotional. Who am I to do this? My child is a drug addict. What type of parent am I? I am not a Bible scholar or preacher. I keep making stupid mistakes as a parent. If I am forgiven, and my sin is forgotten, why do I feel this way? By reading God's word, I realize that my guilt is from not forgiving myself, and my guilt is from the Devil. He wants to steal my joy.

I must forgive myself for the mistakes I have made as a parent and quit wallowing in self-pity and selfish guilt driven thoughts. These thoughts and feelings are not from God. They are from the Devil, the master of lies, the deceiver of truth, the one who seeks to destroy my family and thief of my peace. It states in the second half of

Proverbs 16:6 that "fear of God deflects evil." To be God fearing, I must stay in God's Word often to learn how He parents me. I must place Him first above even my rebellious child.

I must totally give my problems over to God and let Him have control. I must ask and seek His wisdom to be a better parent. I must turn a deaf ear to the devil and only listen to God's word. I must acknowledge that I am a sinner saved by grace through Jesus Christ and that my sins of the past, present, and future are forgiven when I confess my sin. I must seek His forgiveness every day of my existence to keep me from hiding in my own shame. Jesus Christ dealt with my sins once and for all with His own precious life on the cross.

I would be guilty if I had unconfessed sin. I would be guilty if I refused to accept Christ as my Savior. Guilt is a burden we have when we have sinned. I should confess my sins to God and seek His forgiveness. If I have sinned against someone, I should ask for forgiveness. Once I have repented of these things, I should remember that I am free and right before God's eyes. Any further feelings of guilt are from the devil, and should be driven away in God's name! For the Lord Jesus Christ, does not condemn. He provides only conviction that turns me from my sin, draws me closer to Him, and in the end, makes me more like Him.

Dear Lord,

Please forgive my sin and make me white as snow. Please forgive my poor parenting skills and lack of wisdom I have with my child. Restore my relationship with my child. Please remove my guilt and replace it with Your peace and Your love. Grant me wisdom in raising my child. Help me remember how You parent me. Keep the devil away and don't let me listen to his lies. Thank you for sending Your son, Jesus, to take away our sin and restore us to You.

Amen

QUESTIONS FOR THOUGHT:

(1) Am I allowing guilt to consume who I am in God's eyes? Do I truly understand how God sees me?

(2) Have I totally accepted His forgiveness of sin? Have I forgiven myself as God has forgiven me?

(3) Do I realize that if I harbor guilt, I will hide in shame and really never be an effective parent to my child addict?

FORGIVENESS

*"At that point Peter got up the nerve to ask,
"Master, how many times do I forgive
a brother or sister who hurts me?
Seven?" Jesus replied, "Seven! Hardly.
Try seventy times seven."*

— MATTHEW 18: 21-22 THE
MESSAGE

I don't know where to begin with this topic. So, I guess I will just dive in head first. As a parent of a drug addict, there are a lot of things and people that need forgiveness. Sin has a domino effect. Sin does not just affect the person sinning; it affects everyone that person knows and has a relationship with.

During the last several years, I had to ask God to help me forgive:

• My Child: Her choices, disobedience, lies, deceit, disrespect, attitude, and the pain created in my life and my family's life

• Her Friends: Their lack of wisdom, choices, judgment, disobedience, lies, dishonesty and deceitfulness in hiding what was going on with my daughter

• Her School: Their failure to guide my child, their lack of following through with agreements made in parental meetings; teachers just "working a job" and lack of genuine care for an individual; their laziness in fulfilling their responsibilities as educators, counselors, and administrators

• My Friends: I should clarify this one. My real friends have spent time with me, listened and have prayed daily for my daughter and my family. I needed to forgive my social or acquaintance friends for not telling me what was going on or suspected going on until it was too late; afterward their complete withdrawal from me and my daughter. I felt betrayed and like an outcast. I could see the discomfort in their faces if they saw me anywhere. Unfortunately, with drug addiction, people don't know how to approach you. It is viewed by human eyes as a willful sin of the addict. People also judge your skills as a parent. While out in public, I would often hear people talk or expressing concern about other children sick with a disease. It would just hurt because in my case, some people did not know how to communicate about an addict. Instead of stopping to ask about my daughter or our situation, a few friends would just avoid me when they saw me in a public setting.

• My Husband: In dealing with his own pain, I felt neglected at times; In dealing with his own anger, I felt like the one he was angry with at times.

• My Family: My family members are wonderful, godly people and really helped during this trial in our lives, but sometimes opinions were expressed, body language and comments were made that cut to the core of me as a person and a parent. My son loved his sister and is truly a wonderful Christian young man, but sometimes I could just see the anger and dislike he had at times for his sister; sometimes he would try to be disobedient just because it seemed like "she" was getting away with everything.

• My Church: My true friends and church family-the ones that love unconditionally and forgive everything and do not judge, do not gossip or spread rumors I cherish forever. However, some of the people in my church, especially in my daughter's peer group judged my daughter. They pushed her away from God and saw my daughter's sins and problems without removing the "log" in their own eyes. Many excluded my daughter and looked upon her with "haughty" eyes.

• Myself: For somehow failing to meet the needs my

daughter was seeking, and, for being too busy to listen to my daughter. I needed to forgive myself for always having time to give an opinion or throw "the Christian" way of doing things in her face which only drove her further from God. As difficult as it is, I needed to forgive myself for being so angry at the world; angry at God, my family, my husband and totally disliking the people who led my daughter astray or the ones that allowed my daughter to go astray by being silent. I needed to forgive myself for not liking my daughter at times; for not living wholly for God even in the troubled times; for allowing the devil any room to do his dirty work; for being a selfish daughter, daughter-in-law; wife and parent; for not being the Christian example; etc.

In all the sin that was going on in our lives and our tiny world, I could hear God's still small voice speaking: "Forgive them, for they know not what they do!" I remembered all the things Christ had forgiven me of personally in the past. I knew the only way to begin to heal was to forgive the people who directly caused or indirectly caused my pain. I knew that I was full of the world's ways and not God's ways by hanging onto my unforgiveness of others and myself. I have learned the following about forgiveness: Forgiveness is not making light of the offense; Forgiveness is not forgetting what happened. Forgiveness is not reconciliation. Forgiveness is a choice. When I forgave, I was no longer held captive by the offense. When I forgave, I could allow God to heal my heart so that my memory would be without pain and anger. When I forgave, I was freed-my enemies could no longer hold me prisoner. Some relationships have been reconciled while other relationships have become more of a season of my life with no hard feelings and no regret.

It was incredible to feel the weight of the albatross I had hung around my neck lifted when I asked God to help me forgive every person. Notice that I had to ask for help to forgive. It was difficult to ask for forgiveness, but once done, I realized how much time I had wasted just hanging on to all that "sinful" baggage! Forgiveness is not about others, really. It is about being obedient to God! Following in His footsteps! Forgiveness allows me to be a whole person devoted to God. It allows my heart to heal and grow. It strengthens my own personal faith because I realize how much I have been forgiven by God and His amazing sacrifice of His Son in forgiving each of my sins.

Dear Lord,

I think in this whole ordeal; forgiveness was the hardest lesson for me to learn. Yet, it was the most crucial for me to understand and to obey. Thank you that You are the source of forgiveness and that I don't have to rely on my own personal strength and heart to forgive. Thank you for sending Christ to save me from my sins! Thank you for forgiving me!

Amen

QUESTIONS FOR THOUGHT:

(1) Who do I need to forgive?

(2) Have I forgiven myself?

(3) Have I completely accepted God's forgiveness or do I feel the need to crucify Christ repeatedly?

(4) Do I understand what forgiveness is about and will I allow God to help me forgive others and myself?

FEAR

"So do not fear, for I am with you; do not
be dismayed, for I am your God. I will
strengthen you and help you; I will
uphold you with my righteous
right hand"

— ISAIAH 41:10 NIV

Each one of us has something or someone that makes us fearful. Each one of us may react differently to fear based on our own personalities and character. Fear can be a good thing when used to protect us from dangerous situations; fear can be a bad thing especially when it keeps us from doing God's will or causes us not to rely on God when things get a little scary.

Fear tends to gets my heart racing, increases my respiratory rate, causes nausea/vomiting, headaches, breaks me out into a cold sweat, makes me want to run/escape or hide. It can cause me to be hostile and angry. It may cause me to scream or cry. The physical and psychological effects of fear are terrible. If faced with danger like a wild animal or a falling heavy object, I instinctively probably should run. God gave me that to as common sense. However, I do not think God wants me to have irrational fears nor fear what life here on earth may present me with.

Things that I have feared having a drug addict child include: rejection from friends, family, even my daughter; failure of my marriage, fear that my son will turn out the same as my daughter, fear over our finances being exhausted to help my daughter, fear for my health and loved ones' health due to the stress of the situation, and fear that my daughter's actions and addictions will either kill her or someone else. Fear that this problem will never end- that I am stuck with this problem until I die! For me, fear does not mix well with one of my personality traits because I also happen to be a worrier. The two are a bad combination. With four years of worrying about my child and the related fears, I should be crazier than I am. Or I should be dead from physical and psychological ramifications.

Thankfully, by the grace of God, when I fear, He whispers, "Do not be afraid, for I am with you. I will never forsake you or leave you." I find it funny and even maddening at times that He never says the problem will go away. He promises to be our Strength and carry us when we cannot handle any more fear and challenges. I firmly believe God is in the miracle business, and that He can do anything to change the situation. I also know, beyond a shadow of a doubt, that if my situation never changes, He will remain the same. Therefore, I shouldn't be afraid. I guess I am like Peter when he walked on water with Jesus. For a moment, he had no fear, but let his faith in God lead him through an impossible feat. But, when he relied on himself and took his eyes off Christ, he became fearful; he doubted, and he sank. Fortunately, God never changes. He keeps on loving and believing in you and I as He did Peter. He kept sustaining Peter in difficulties, and eventually carried him home to glory, as He will do for you and I.

To combat fear, I must keep my eyes on Jesus. Additionally, I must not make my fears bigger than my God. I must take captive my thoughts and feelings and remember God's word and His promises. I must accept that God will be with me even when I walk in the valley. I must grasp because of what Christ did on the cross that I am eternally protected, and my child is eternally protected.

One day I will grow into a fearless woman of God. God's not done with me yet! And, I have a lot of spiritual growing to do. My prayer is that if you are a parent out there and you are experiencing these same fears, you will let God be your Hero and your Savior. I pray that you will face the problems and concerns with a firm affirmation that God is carrying you and upholding you with His hand.

Dear Lord,

I ask that you remove fear from me in Jesus name. Be my strength and uphold me when I can't see past my fears. Let me see and feel Your presence. Hold me when I am shaking and frozen with fear. Sustain and strengthen me. Send peace and give me Eternal perspective. Thank you that nothing can ever separate You from me.

Amen

QUESTIONS FOR THOUGHT:

- What do I fear the most in this battle of addiction with my child?
- What does God say about fear? Have I looked in the Bible at all the verses about fear and let them settle over me?
- Can I let go of my fear and give it to God to handle? Will I allow God to strengthen me and uphold me by submitting my fear?
- As a child of God do I acknowledge that nothing can separate me from God? That this present

world is only a vapor, my home is in Heaven, and God has already won the battle? Or, that even if the worst happens, God will always be here with me until He calls me home to Heaven? Or, that God has a place for me and my child in Heaven? Do I have this Eternal perspective to focus on when everything else here seems so scary?

STRENGTH

*"It is strength that endures the
unendurable and spills over into joy,
thanking the Father who makes us
strong enough to take part in
everything bright and beautiful that he
has for us,"*

— COLOSSIANS 1:12 THE
MESSAGE

Human strength increases when we actively use our muscles in a way that combines power, force, and adequate load. Strength increases over time and requires consistent efforts on at least a weekly basis. It is also interesting to note our bodies will find the most efficient way to perform a task; therefore, once in a strength training program, it is easy to plateau if we do the same training day after day. A good strength program allows for muscle confusion to provide growth and gains. Thus, a variety of movements, loads at different angles, and speed help to produce a strong muscle. But what about our emotional and spiritual strength? How do we get stronger in these very relevant areas of our life?

Our Father in Heaven tells us many times in His Word He is the source of our strength. The Bible also states God's strength "comes into its own in our weakness" (2 Corinthians 9-10 The Message Bible). Like strength training, spiritual strength comes with consistency; which is time spent in our relationship with Christ. In contrast, with physical strengthening, we are usually to some extent in control with the situation and progression (although some feats of physical strength can only be explained by God). With spiritual strengthening, we are not in control. We have no strength on our own. We are weak. The only tool we have to strengthen ourselves is the utter and complete submission of ourselves and our situation to Christ, our Lord. That submission also includes a complete focus on Christ, obedience to His Word and His direction. Similar to physical strengthening, spiritual strengthening can be anguishing, produce pain, cause you to fall on your face, and cause opposition in our human realm. It can come at you in many forms. It allows no room for a plateau. It can hit you from any angle and confuse the heck out of you.

Thankfully, just as physical training produces outward and inward effects, spiritual strengthening reveals God's glory inside and out. Spiritual strengthening allows us to become more like Christ.

The challenges that come with a loving a drug addict made me realize I was weak, not only physically and mentally, but spiritually. I tried to handle everything myself. If only I could be the perfect parent, discipline more, be a better example, be a better leader, be a better advisor, be more understanding, be tougher, be stronger, then I could make my child behave how she should, and I could make her stop using drugs. Even though I was using various parenting skills, angles, strategies, and force, I could not handle the burden of raising a child addict. Relief came when my husband and I invested time with various trainers such as grandparents, Christian friends, our pastor, and even medical/psychological professionals. At first, we gained strength from the use of these sources. Some of what was suggested worked, but these ultimately failed to fuel our strength in the long run. God had to become our strength in our weakness! My husband and I had to surrender everything including our daughter to Him.

With my daughter's drug addiction, I was brought to my knees! One of our most fearful times occurred after the line had finally been drawn in our household rules. My daughter had been caught again with drugs and arrested by the police. We, as a family, including my daughter (in a round- about-way) agreed through God's heavy direction she had to leave home and attend a Christian intervention program for teens. I was so fearful and scared. I thought how Abraham must have felt when God asked him to sacrifice his only son, or the way Samson felt when the one he loved cut off his source of strength! I was weak. I didn't think I could handle it. How can a father have the strength to fly thousands of miles away from home with his daughter and just leave her there with strangers? How can a mother stand to watch her child go without knowing if she will ever come back? How can a married couple sustain the "the love of their love" being gone? How can parents be strong for their other child while that sibling is at a loss for his big sister?

The Lord showed me Colossians 1:12. The answer is in the verse above! Total submission and reliance on God allow my source of strength to grow. It is important to remember even though our physical and emotional weaknesses in this world may never change, God's Glory will ultimately triumph and my spiritual strength can increase. Consistent prayer and time spent focusing on my relationship with Christ instead of my heartache, pain, failures, and weakness become my "personal trainer," as a result, my spiritual strength will flourish. I remember to look for God in the midst of my shortcomings. It may come in simple ways such as "thinking of you" cards in the mail; "how are you doing" phone calls or texts; or plainly written words only God meant for my blind eyes to see. One way God reached out to us happened on my husband's way to the Christian Intervention program for teens. My husband and I were so scared if we were doing the right thing. While on the bus taking my daughter to her destination, my husband noticed a sign over the bus driver's head. The sign read: "Your courtesy driver today is Jesus"! Hallelujah! It was a simple sign, actually the name of the bus driver; but to us, it was God's way of showing up at our weakest moment. God had just provided us with the strength to leave our daughter in His hands and the hands of Christian strangers.

Just as building human strength takes time, so does building spiritual strength. It cannot be done overnight or in just a few weeks. I realize it will probably take a lifetime. But, my Heavenly Father is my source of strength, and He will conquer all my weaknesses! He will provide me with strength and He will sustain me through this battle with drug addiction. He will help me endure the unendurable-His power and control will be delivered as I submit everything unto Him. He will bless me with a strong spirit-full of joy and thankfulness in an otherwise impossible situation.

Dear Lord,

Thank you for being my source of strength. Thank you that it may only be the strength to breathe in and out! Thank you for being there. Thank you for silencing my fears! Thank you for letting me yell and cry, but then pulling me out of the pit! Forgive me when I lose my focus on You and have a pity party or a panic attack instead. Thank you for Christian family and friends those You send to help keep me strong. Thank you for being so obvious when I am blind. Thank you for who You are. Thank you for showing up and showing out! Thank you that even though the physical pain and sadness of my weakness are present, your strength gives me power and joy for the future You control!

Amen

QUESTIONS FOR THOUGHT:

- Do I depend on my strength to fight this battle of addiction with my child or am I relying on God for my source of strength?
- Am I strong Spiritually?
- How can I improve my Spiritual strength and ignore the weakness I feel physically, mentally and emotionally?

SPIRITUAL WARFARE

"He said, 'Don't worry about it-there are more on our side than on their side.' Then Elisha prayed, 'O God, open his eyes and let him see.' The eyes of the young man were opened, and he saw. A wonder! The whole mountainside full of horses and chariots of fire surrounding Elisha!"

— 2 KINGS 6:16-17 THE MESSAGE

I previously heard of spiritual warfare, but never experienced it until my daughter hit the age of 16 years-old when her drug issue reached a fever pitch. Time has passed; and as much as I hate it, our family is still in the midst of spiritual warfare. I guess everyone is in the middle of spiritual warfare whether it be a battle with drugs, alcohol, finances, disease, or whatever the devil is doing here on Earth to win non-Christians to his side or to steal the joy and create doubt in the faith of Christians.

Through the last four years, we have had tough battles with my daughter's rebellious nature and her addiction to drugs. We have had victories over these issues. We had times of peace, joy and times when everything in the world was right (a little Heaven on Earth). But, the Devil is still prowling. He waits when we are weak or when we are so comfortable with our situation to pounce- to engage in battle again!

It says in Revelations, chapter 12 verse 4: "The Dragon crouched before the Woman in childbirth, poised to eat up the Child when it came" (The Message). The Devil is in an all-out war with God. He is here on Earth trying his best to recruit to his army and kill/ destroy those who are of God. He is trying his best to kill our daughter with drugs and with a rebellious spirit. She is a Christian, but she is in bondage because of the drugs. She is full of shame, pain, and self-loathing. It has made her faith weak.

She has attempted to give this stronghold over to God, but this sin, this god of her life the devil keeps throwing her way, grabs her every time. She has brief periods of victory over evil, but I think she is a lot like Elisha's servant in 2 Kings. She has little faith and can't see the angel armies surrounding her. She has forgotten to wear the armor of God. In her drug depraved mind, she feels unworthy of anything God would have for her.

Likewise, as parents, we have been blind to "the mountainside full of horses and chariots of fire surrounding" us. Instead, we believe the devil's lies that we are fighting alone in a no-win situation. Unfortunately, we also have been found unprepared for the battle in front of us-found with no weapons or protection. As a parent of a drug addict, I have let my body and my soul (my mind, will, and emotions) grow louder than my Spirit. Watching my child suffer drug addiction causes pain both physically and emotionally within me. Fear of the unknown overtakes me. Doubt drowns me.

Ephesians 6:10 speaks about the Armor of God. We are to shield ourselves with Truth, Righteousness, Peace, Faith, and Salvation. It says we are to apply them not just hear the words. I think I have applied salvation, truth, and righteousness; but I keep forgetting to fasten faith and peace to myself. These two parts seem to keep falling off. Instead, I wear doubt, and I wear fear.

I am listening to the lies of the devil. But God calls me to be a mighty warrior for Him. In this same chapter of Ephesians, it states God's Word is an indispensable weapon, and prayer is essential in this never-ending battle. I must learn to grab these weapons first, instead of reacting after the devil has sent his first attack.

I have learned even though God has the ultimate victory, I still have my battle responsibilities. God has given me everything I need to fight from victory not to victory. One of my biggest responsibilities in this spiritual warfare is for me to take every thought captive and align it with the Word of God. Spending time daily with God and studying His Word is such a strong fortress to be used as a parent of a drug addict. I must not listen to what the devil says nor let my feelings overwhelm me. I must seize and use the weapon of prayer always. I must pray without a doubt and claim God's promises through Scripture over every situation this demon of drug addiction throws at me. I must realize angel armies surround me and they outnumber those of the enemy.

I am learning to be a mighty warrior for God. I hope my daughter will learn to be a mighty warrior for God just as He has called me to be. I pray she will quit letting the devil hold her as a prisoner of war because she is not his- she is a Child of God. I know ultimately the battle will be won and His Glory and Power will reign forever. In the meantime, I have only to take my marching orders and to obey my Commanding Officer for He is the Victor! He is in control! He will not be defeated!

Dear Lord,

I ask you forgive me for not being prepared for battle. I ask you to forgive me for retreating or going AWOL in this war I seem unable to control. I ask You to keep me centered and focused on you, your word, and always connected with prayer. I ask that, when I doubt or am afraid, You will show me your strength somehow. I ask you keep me prepared before the trouble comes and I will still be standing when it is passed. Remind me to take my thoughts captive and to align my defense to Your Word and promises. Thank you for having the final say in this world and victory over evil.

Amen

ADDITIONAL SCRIPTURE REFERENCES:

> *"Be prepared. You're up against far more than you can handle on your own. Take all the help you can get, every weapon God has issued, so that when it's all over but the shouting you'll still be on your feet."*

> — EPHESIANS 6:13 THE MESSAGE

QUESTIONS FOR THOUGHT:

- Am I applying the Armor of God to myself each day-all of it not parts and pieces?

- Do I acknowledge God as the ultimate victor, that He is fighting my battles and surrounds me with His angel armies?
- Do I realize some of the things in this world, especially drug addiction are a part of spiritual warfare and I desperately need to be in God's Word and in constant prayer to be a mighty warrior for God?
- Do I cast off fear and doubt? Do I take my thoughts captive and align them with God's Word and promises?

WORRY AND ANXIETY

"Don't fret or worry. Instead of worrying, pray. Let petitions and praises shape your worries into prayers, letting God know your concerns. Before you know it, a sense of God's wholeness, everything coming together for good, will come and settle you down. It's wonderful what happens when Christ displaces worry at the center of your life"

— PHILIPPIANS 4: 6-7 THE MESSAGE

I am by nature a worrier. I worry about everything. I have wasted a lot of time just worrying. God gave me a husband that handles worrying beautifully, and my husband has helped to balance my tendency to worry.

God worked on my worrying and continued to use my husband to help me through it. Because, if not, with all that has come with our wayward child and the shackles of addiction, I would be insane right now.

Proverbs 12:25 says worry weighs us down. Before long, worrisome thoughts become irrational thoughts and manifest themselves into physical symptoms of sickness and disease.

Things I have worried about over my child addict have included:

• What if she dies?

• What if she gets arrested?

• What if she refuses treatment?

• What if she gets an illness because of her drug addiction?

• What if we run out of money trying to help her?

• What if my marriage won't survive this ordeal?

• What if she doesn't get better?

• What if my family thinks we are wrong in our approach to help our daughter?

And the list goes on.

The funny thing is some of what I worried about happened. She was arrested several times. She got illnesses from her risky behaviors with drug addiction. We did nearly lose all our financial means in trying to help her recover. And, she is not any better. I worried for nothing really. These things happened, but God helped my family and me through each one of these trials. The worrying was a waste. What I should have been doing more of was praying. I prayed, but I think I worried more than I prayed.

I still worry about some of the other things, especially about what if she dies? But, as soon as the thought comes to my mind, I focus on God. I know He loves her far more than I even do, and He will do what is best for her. My husband and I have come to terms her death may happen. Not all things end the way we want them to, but we have decided God will get the Glory even through her death if that were to happen. We will not let the Devil and the evil he has thrown at our family win. That determination is a worry stopper for sure. The battle is won no matter what!

The worst things I worry about may come true, or they may not come true. Either way, God deserves the Glory, because He will be there to walk through the fire with me. He will rescue me from defeat. He is greater than my worst worry and fear. He is writing the story, and it will eventually end good, even if it differs significantly from what I envisioned.

Having a child or loved one as an addict, is no fun. That person never knows the turmoil he or she is causing in the other person's life. God knows the turmoil I am experiencing though, and He does not want my life to be consumed with anxiousness and fear. He wants me to know and believe in Him, to trust Him no matter what the outcome may be. I am to cast my fears and anxious thoughts onto Him. I am to ask Him to fill me with His power, strength, and peace. I am to call upon His name when anxious thoughts overtake me. Give praise unto Him that delivers me and gives me supernatural strength!

To drop to my knees before the Lord; to give Him praise and let my petitions be known to Him is the way to go. He will displace the worry. He will replace it with His goodness; His mercy; and His peace. My circumstance may not change, but He is the victor over evil. He will fight out battles right alongside me and will carry me when I can no longer fight. Worry not! Pray more! Seek the presence of the Lord.

Dear Lord,

Forgive my worrying. Call me onto you when I worry. Turn my mind and heart towards you. I will praise you when I fear and turn my petitions to your ear. Thank you for hearing me and for turning my worry into focus on You. You are working for my good. Things may or may not happen. My job is to stay focused on you and not the "what ifs."

Amen

ADDITIONAL SCRIPTURE REFERENCES:

"Give your entire attention to what God is doing right now and don't get worked up about what may or may not happen tomorrow. God will help you deal with whatever hard things come up when the time comes."

— MATTHEW 6:34 THE MESSAGE

QUESTIONS FOR THOUGHT:

- When I worry, do I realize I am belittling my faith and not trusting God?
- If I am not willing to submit my problems to God, am I capable of taking responsibility for everything drug addiction will throw my way? If I am not capable of handling it why can't I give it to the One who is capable of handling it?
- How is my fretting over a situation or issue about my drug addict child going to change the circumstance? If there is something I can do to help, am I seeking God for wisdom and being active in His strength to carry out the task? If it is an issue, I have no control over why do I persist in carrying the burden? Who can carry the weight?

SLEEPLESSNESS

*If I am sleepless at midnight, I spend the
hours in grateful reflection. Because
you've always stood up for me, I'm free
to run and play. I hold onto you for
dear life and you hold me steady
as post.*

— PSALM 63: 6-8 THE MESSAGE

The trials I have been through with my daughter over the last few years caused me to lose a lot of sleep. Bad habits such as worrying, replaying arguments in my mind, and over-thinking, caused me to develop full-blown insomnia. I would go days sometimes 4-5 days in a row without sleeping more than an hour or two each night. I even dreaded nightfall because I knew I would be miserable again and not sleep.

The lack of sleep caused me to develop anxiety and depression, have mood swings, lack of energy, and inability to form clear thoughts. Often, I would forget things I would normally remember. It seemed I was always sick and I was out of my body's natural rhythm. The fact was, I was so miserable, I eventually went to the doctor about my insomnia. My doctor put me on medicine because of the unhealthy state I was in physically and emotionally.

The medicine helped for a while, but I had a tough time getting off medication. While I had restored my sleep pattern and could function again as a human, a wife, mom, and as an employee, I knew I did not want to be on the sleep medicine forever. But as soon as I would try to come off the medication, something would happen with my daughter again with the drugs and the rebellion.

I would end up not being able to sleep and having to take the sleep medicine. It was becoming a crutch I no longer wanted with me!! After two years of trying to stop taking the sleep medicine, God got my attention during a twenty-one-day of prayer and fasting event we had at our church. God showed me the things that were causing me to lose sleep were also taking my focus off of Him.

What I was doing was worrying, thinking negatively, hanging on to anger, holding onto fear and doubt, and not surrendering everything to Him. I knew each one of these things I was doing was wrong and I was not walking my talk. I was not living out my faith and beliefs. I was thinking of having faith. I was talking about having faith. But, I was not acting on faith the way God wanted me to. He wanted me to surrender everything, including what I was thinking about at night, and what dreams would jolt me awake at night, He wanted me to give them to Him.

During the twenty-one-day of prayer and fasting, I learned I had to cling on to God. I replaced my thoughts and desires with His thoughts and desires. I replaced worry with trust. I replaced anger with forgiveness. I replaced fear and doubt with peace and conquered victory. I replaced negative thinking with thanksgiving. At the end of the twenty-one-day of prayer, God showed me through depending on Him in my weaknesses, He could accomplish what needed to be done. My initial desire during prayer and fasting was to see a change in my daughter. By the end of the 21 days, God showed me I needed to change some things in my life.

My daughter's rebellion and addiction remained unchanged for now for a reason only my God knows. Remarkably, I could change and live by faith. I can sleep now. It is not perfect rest, but it is not like horrible insomnia I had experienced. I still get those human thoughts of worry, negative thinking, and anger at night that want to keep me up. But now instead of dwelling on them, I pray to God. I meditate on the goodness of God! I worship Him in my sleeplessness and before I know it I am resting peacefully in His loving arms in the midst of a painful time in my life!

Dear Lord,

Thank you for using the twenty-one-day of prayer and fasting to change me. Thank you for showing me how staying close to you and giving everything to you will bring me rest even though the circumstance has not changed. Thank you that I can spend time with you when I am restless and cannot sleep. Thank you that in Your presence I can find rest.

Amen

QUESTIONS FOR THOUGHT:

- What is causing my sleeplessness? Worry? Fear? My own irrational thoughts?
- What good is it doing me to lie in bed and hang on to these "sleep stealers"? Have I gotten up and engaged God with my sleeplessness?
- Am I resting in His presence or am I consumed with my own thoughts and my own crazy presence?

PAIN AND SUFFERING

*"What did I do to deserve this? Did I ever
hit anyone who was calling for help?
Haven't I wept for those who live a
hard life, been heartsick over the lot of
the poor? But where did it get me? I
expected good, but evil showed up. I
looked for light, but darkness fell."*

— JOB 30: 24-26 THE MESSAGE

Job was a good man, and he loved God. At one
point, he had it all: friends, good family, health,
and wealth. But, Job was not perfect, and neither
was his family. Job made sacrificial atonements,
not only for his personal sins, but for the sins of his family,
and for any sins they may commit. He was obedient to

God and tried his best to follow God's ways. Yet, he lost everything. He lost his children, his wealth, his health, and his influence in society.

Now, I have not had it as bad as Job, but I suffered to some extent, and I understand to a degree where Job is coming from. I lost the child I once knew to drugs. Friends abandoned me. I was shunned by people in public places because I am a parent of an "addict" child. I have been physically and mentally sick from the sheer exhaustion resulting from trying to parent a drug abusing child. I have been put under financial strain. I experienced anguish and pain.

I experienced suffering for which I did not understand the reason behind it. It would be ok to have this pain if I had been a bad person or committed some terrible act. I am by no means perfect and without sin, but when I sin or realize I have sinned, I try to ask for forgiveness as quick as possible. I try to do well as a person. So, I, like Job, asked God, "Why, God? Why did this happen? Haven't I been good and done what you asked of me? Why is my child slowly killing herself? Why is my child turning away from her family? Why is my child wayward from You?"

I love Job's comments in chapter 29:1-6,

"Oh, how I long for the good old days, when God took such good care of me... Oh, how I miss those golden years when God's friendship graced my home, When the Mighty One

was still by my side, and my children were all around me,
when everything was going my way, and nothing seemed
too difficult."

I miss those days. I get sad when I think back to how
things were. How did things go so wrong? Get so off
track? I too have a "face blotched red from weeping and
dark shadows under my eyes" just as Job states in Job
16:16. And yes, like Job said many times, I hate my life- as
a parent of an addict. I, like Job, wanted answers from
God and was laying it all out on the table. There is a part
of Job's story I was not aware of. In the book of Job, from
the very beginning, God is in full control and is fully
victorious. The part of Job's story and my story I was
unaware of, is there is real spiritual warfare out there. The
Devil is out fighting against God and the people of God
every day. However, God is victorious over the devil.
Sometimes my human life is caught up in this spiritual
warfare. For reasons I do not understand, the devil makes
his strike out of nowhere. It seems God is not to be found
anywhere. But God has won the battle, and His angel
armies are all around me fighting against things I do not
comprehend.

As a human, I do not understand the battles being played
out in the heavenly realms. God uses those actions and the
human suffering I entail to carry out His successful plan.
God's very own son suffered more than any human could,
and His son was perfect, utterly blameless. Jesus

experienced immense pain, suffering, and separation from God, but I believe Christ could see the spiritual battle before Him and the victory that was ahead of Him. Christ knew those same feelings I go through when I am suffering. He even asks for "the cup to be removed." Yet, Christ knew God's will and Christ yielded to the Father's plan for His life because He knew the outcome of the battle.

Job couldn't see he was in the middle of a spiritual battle between the devil and God until God spoke to Job in a storm. Refer to Job chapters 38-41. Job realized God is always there. God was and is in complete control of the Universe. God is victorious over the devil. God's plan will be completed at all costs. I think Job realized there was far more going on in the spiritual realms than he could have understood. Job recognized God's ways are beyond what the human mind can comprehend. Job did not see the whole picture in the midst of his suffering. Once God opened Job's eyes to His majestic ways, Job worshipped God and asked for forgiveness for not understanding God's ways.

Do I think it's okay to question God about our suffering? Yes! Job did. David did. Many other followers of God did. But, I understand in the midst of my pain and suffering and uncomfortable circumstances, I must realize God is greater than addiction. God is bigger than the suffering and pain I am experiencing. I must know God is not picking on my family and me. I must acknowledge there are battles in the Heavenly realms being fought and won that I don't even know about. I should know life will not be easy. Suffering must come. I must, in the midst of suffering, draw as close to God as I can and to know He has got this. I may ask "why" but conclude with "You have my family and me in the palm of your loving hand."

Dear Lord,

Thank you that you are a God I can ask and talk to about anything. Thank you that I can ask questions and make my requests known to you. Thank you that you know my thoughts before I even get them out of my mouth. Please help me God in this suffering and pain that I feel as I watch my child ruin her life with drugs. Thank you for fighting battles for me I don't even know about Lord. Thank you that you know how this will end and it is all a part of your plan. Thank you that I have a place called Heaven where I will suffer no more. Thank you that You are always present no matter when pain and suffering make me feel you are not. Those are just mere feelings and not the truth. Thank you that whatever I am going through as a parent of an addict you will one day turn it all around, and your great plan will be revealed.

Amen

QUESTIONS FOR THOUGHT:

- Why do I think this world should be perfect and my life should be easy?
- Do I not know this world is temporary and Heaven is for eternity?
- Do I understand God is always present even when I allow my pain and suffering to become so big I can't feel God's presence?
- Do I submit that God's ways are not my ways, His thoughts not my thoughts?
- Do I believe God is a good God and there are things in the spiritual realm I cannot understand, but God sees the whole picture and is working for the good of those who love Him?
- Do I realize God does not cause pain and suffering, but God sometimes allows pain and suffering to produce something for the greater good of mankind and to bring Glory unto Him?
- Do I know I can reach out to others suffering from similar situations and bring not only them peace and joy but peace and joy for myself?
- Do I know if I worship God in the midst of my pain and suffering they will "grow strangely dim" in the light of who God is?

APATHETIC AND EMPTY

"A thief is only there to steal and kill and
destroy. I came so they can have real
and eternal life, more and better life
than they ever dreamed of."

— JOHN 10:10 THE MESSAGE

If any of you had a wayward child, you might well know the feeling of apathy, a sense of pure emptiness. No matter what you do, you are butting your head against the wall. With an addict, the rebellion intensifies. You ignore the feeling of the rejection and hurt you first felt when your child went against your ways. Instead, you grow numb. You seem to not care just to avoid the pain. The "whatever" mode of thinking sets in.

It is numbness full of selfishness. This apathy is worldly, and it shows a pure lack of faith.

During this apathetic time in my life, I wanted to blame my child for making me have this lack of feeling- this emptiness. After all, I would never have felt this way if she had not kept being rebellious. Wrong! This emptiness and apathy are straight from the devil himself, who came to steal, kill, and destroy my faith and my joy. And I am responsible for leaving the door open for this notorious thief. I let my feelings of depression, sadness, anger, resentment fill me to the brim. In fact, I let myself believe the devil's lie and let that snake steal my focus away from the Source of my inner most being-who I am in Christ!

Yes, I was not happy with the way my child was choosing to behave, and I had a right to be angry. I had a reason to be frustrated. But, I did not have the right to be apathetic! I did not have to right to be lukewarm about the situation. What I should have done was look up! My focus should have been on my Lord, who is big enough for my problems. He never left and never quit working on my problems. Yes, I was living in chaos and misery in my household, but my God was right there holding my hand. It was going to be in His timing to work things out not just for me, but for the one who needed Him the most, my daughter. Instead, I let the Devil fill me with doubt and emptiness every time things went wrong. I believed the devil's lie that things would never change and why should I care.

God does not want my life to be void, full of apathy and emptiness. I needed to get on my knees and pray! I had to admit whatever I was feeling to God because He understands. He wants to listen, no matter what I am thinking and feeling. He wants me to trust Him and to lay my feelings and concerns at the cross. Now, things may not get better, things may not change, or may change then get worse again. But, I can't become numb in my faith! I must look up! I must draw a line in the sand and quit listening and believing Satan's lies. The times I don't think God is there, I keep breathing and remembering where that breath comes from. I must remember His grace is sufficient! Above all else, I must pray without ceasing and cast all my worries on Him. I may have to be still sometimes, but I don't have to be numb and empty. I think God would rather me be frustrated, yet focused on Him. I may be scared and tired of the battle, but I am focused on my Commanding Officer and following through to the bitter end, win or lose! I will not allow the devil to steal, kill and destroy, for Christ came that I may have life and live it to the full!

Dear Lord,

Thank you for allowing time to work through my problems in my family. Thank you for allowing me time to see Your glorious work! Forgive my apathetic feelings and doubt that things would ever change. Thank you for not "spewing me out of your mouth" like I deserved!

Thank you for feelings no matter how painful they are sometimes! Keep me guarded against my feelings especially those desperate feelings! Let those types of feelings sound an alarm that You are a faithful Redeemer of all! Do not let me be directed by my feelings. Help me to choose not to listen to the devil's lies. Help me to choose the life You came to give, and my feelings will follow. I thank you that I can experience a full life in the midst of a debilitating storm because I am anchored in You.

Amen

ADDITIONAL SCRIPTURE REFERENCES:

"The thief comes only to steal and kill and destroy; I have come that they may have life and have it to the full"

— JOHN 10:10 NIV

QUESTIONS FOR THOUGHT:

- Have I allowed the chaos from having a child drug addict to settle in a state of apathy and emptiness?

- Have I given up on my child, and even worse, have I given up on God?
- Do I realize who the real culprit is in this horrible situation and why do I allow myself to sit at the devil's table instead of me dining with my Jesus?
- Can I ask God to clear my eyes; open my ears; and cleanse my calloused heart, so I may live fully even in the midst of a crisis?

WHERE ARE YOU, GOD?

*"God, God... my God! Why did you dump
me miles from nowhere: Doubled up
with pain, I call to God all the day
long. No answer. Nothing. I keep at it
all night, tossing and turning"*

— PSALM 22:1-2 THE MESSAGE

I must ask a question: Have you ever been in the midst of needing an answer to a problem or needing help with an issue and it seems like God is out to lunch? That is a rather rough question for a so-called Christian to be asking, isn't it? If each of us were honest, we have all asked God a similar question.

Sometimes it's like God is far away; but, I am the one not

near Him in a relationship. I have gone my way and left God out of the equation. It only seems like He is not there. In fact, He has and is there all along. I am guilty of walking away from God. He's never abandoned me. In other cases, it seems everything I am doing is in line with God. I am praying, studying His Word, trying to do the best I can. Yet, the answer does not come, or the solution to a problem or issue will not reveal itself.

During the years my family has been plagued with a child battling drug addiction, I have often felt like God was far away. It has been well over four years since all this drug addiction nightmare began with my child. Sometimes our prayers were answered immediately and other times when prayers just seemed to go unheard or ignored by God. I sometimes just thought God would let us figure this out on our own. Over the last few years, I have questioned God and this plan He had for my life. This did not seem to fit the "Christian Plan" for my family. We were supposed to have the Cinderella story not a complete nightmare of a family life. I guess somewhere in my tiny brain, I thought everything would continue to be smooth sailing in life and "these types of things" only happen to those who needed to get back on track or to those who just did not follow God.

No way would I ever say we were the perfect Christian family! We all fall short and seek our own way. But, compared to the world's standards, we surely assumed we had it right. So, when we began to first have trouble with our daughter and her drug issues, we prayed. We prayed for her to turn away from this sin and prayed God would change her life. We prayed for a rededication of her life to God since she was already a Christian. At times, prayers seemed to be heard, and we thought she was getting it right. She even thought she was getting it right with God, but would eventually fall off the wagon and return to the monster of drugs ruling her life. We prayed. We prayed again and again. We had our whole extended family and closest friends praying. Even strangers were praying. But, we did not see a total deliverance and things seemed to get worse; family fights, police calls to the house, minor arrests for under-age drinking, drug use, etc. Out of complete desperation, I screamed at God. "*Why* is this happening? Where are You? Do You hear me? Answer this prayer now!" That all sounds like a modern-day psalm from David, doesn't it?

I feel like I am trying and doing everything God wants me to do in this situation. I know well He can heal this disease in an instant or at least sometime soon, but the answer just has not come yet. Thinking and asking God this question makes me feel doubt and makes me feel crummy about myself as a Christian. I should not be asking God this! I know He is there, and I know He loves me! He died on the Cross for me what more should I ask, right?

These feelings have gnawed at my gut for years now. Not that along the way during all these years God has not shown Himself to me or let me know He was there. He by far has done that time after time, through friends He has provided for me; through messages in Scripture, through sermons on Sunday mornings, even through strangers on the street. It might be a kind word. It might be a special verse someone sends. It might be a stranger or friend telling me their story about how addiction affected them and how God came through for them. I have had God moments. Yet, my prayer or my problem has not been fixed yet. I often thought, when is it going to be my miracle, my answered prayer? I even thought, well this is God's will for my life. I might as well just accept it. But, I cannot seem to do that at all! That belief goes against everything I know and believe about God. I don't believe God would want my daughter to be an addict and our family to suffer the way it has for this long.

Then one day, I realized where the problem lies. My human needs to have this pain taken away have impeded me believing God has and will answer my prayer one day. He has never been "out to lunch" about my daughter's addiction and issues. I have been "to lunch" way too often with my problem. He has been, is, and will be right there with us for as long as it takes for His greatest glory and plans to be revealed.

A recent sermon from an associate pastor at my church confirmed to me I had to decide God would answer my prayer. I had to believe my daughter would be delivered from addiction to the saving grace of God. I had to thank

God for the miracle He already was doing in my life and in her life. I had to continue to be faithful in what I could not yet see. I believe in a God I cannot see. I believe in a Heaven I cannot see. If I can believe in those, I can believe His plan for my daughter and for me is only the best. I can believe He will finish what He started. I can believe He is right here with me carrying me to a place of healing, peace, and love.

I also needed to reflect on who God was and what He had done for me. I knew my God was Great. I knew He had helped me with things in the past. I had seen Him work miracles in my family's life and in the life of my friends and in my patients. I knew He had saved me and I was a child of God. I just continued to breathe in and out; continued to study His word; continued to pray; continued to remember God would answer my prayer in His timing (even if I were in the grave). I continued to believe God would conquer all evil, and to know all healing would occur in Heaven if not on this Earth.

Dear Lord,

Thank you for being there! Thank you for allowing me to ask why? Thank you that you have provided examples of people in the Bible you dearly love that asked you the same question I did. Thank you for showing David's openness with you in your word. Thank you for Christ's close relationship with you. Both men in the midst of humanness, pain, and grief felt forsaken; yet they were not! You completed in them what you started. Thank you for the miracle of healing you are doing in my life and in my child's life. For Yours is the power and glory forever.

Amen

ADDITIONAL SCRIPTURE REFERENCES:

> *"God, how long do I have to cry out for help before you listen? How many times do I have to yell, "Help! Murder! Police!" before you come to the rescue?"*

> — HABAKKUK 1:2 THE MESSAGE

QUESTIONS FOR THOUGHT:

- Is it okay for me to question God? It is it okay for me to cry out to Him in anguish and despair?
- Do I truly believe God is hearing my prayer and working on the answer in His timing? Or, do I believe the God that sent His one and only Son to die on the cross for me would care so little about me? Does it make sense if He would let his

Son die on my behalf that He would ignore me or leave me? Then, why do I think that?

- Am I trying to make God work on my timeline when He is the author and controller of time?
- Can I trust the length of time; the waiting and silence are all in God's hands and deliverance will come at the perfect time?

LACK OF FAITH

"Jesus said, 'If? There are no 'ifs' among believers. Anything can happen. No sooner were the words out of his mouth than the father cried, 'Then I believe. Help me with my doubts!'"

— MARK 9: 23-24 THE MESSAGE

As a parent of a child who struggles with drug addiction, I saw my child wither away physically. I noticed the change in my child's cognitive processes and experienced the emotional and behavioral changes in my child. Even worse, I suffered the loss of relationship with my child. It is gut-wrenching to watch all these terrible things happen; the physical, mental, emotional and spiritual illness addiction has created in my child. It is as if my child has been possessed by something that cannot be expelled. I am literally watching my child commit slow suicide, and I can do nothing to stop it.

As a parent of a drug-addicted child, I have prayed and prayed for God to heal my daughter of addiction. I have had numerous prayer warriors pray for her. I have sent her to several rehabs, doctors, and counselors. I have experienced the pain of giving "tough love" to my daughter hoping she would come to her senses one day.

After I did all I knew to do and the answer to my prayer seemed so distant or not likely to happen, I doubted if God was listening. I heard stories of miraculous healing from drug addiction. If God did that for one person, maybe He would do that for my daughter. But, that was not and is not the way God is working in this process. This process has been a test of my faith. To be honest, my faith had been found lacking.

Deep down, I knew God had to be listening and had to be working behind the scenes in ways I could not see or understand. But, there were days where it seemed everything was coming apart at the seams. There were days when I thought nothing would ever get better. Sometimes it seems I could not continue, and I would tell God, "If you would heal her, everything would be okay!"

God showed me a verse: Mark 9:24. It hit home with me. In this chapter, a father is asking Jesus to heal his son from a demon that has possessed him since he was a young child. The father asks Jesus (in verse twenty-two), "If you can do anything do it. Have a heart and help us". Jesus replies to the father that believers have no "ifs" when they seek God because anything can happen. The father exclaims he believes. Then, the father asked Jesus to help him with his unbelief.

So, like this father in Mark, I will believe God will heal my daughter one day in His way and in His timing. I will ask God to help me with my doubts. If you continue to read Mark chapter 9, through verse 29, you discover prayer is very important in the healing process as well. So I will not quit praying! I will continue to PUSH: Pray Until Something Happens. This is an acronym a former addict gave my husband to remember. As I am going through this trial, it is just another great reminder through another human being that God is there and is faithful.

Dear Lord,

Please forgive my disbelief. Please help me not to doubt especially when all hell breaks loose when the battles against addiction seem to be lost. Thank you for answering my call. Give me peace and reassurance while I am waiting.

Amen

QUESTIONS FOR THOUGHT:

- Do I have "ifs" when I pray to Jesus to heal my child of addiction and rescue my family from the effects of addiction?
- Do I take my stand as a believer that I really cannot doubt what my almighty God can do? Do I claim my Savior can do anything?
- Have I obeyed the Lord's command to trust Him and believe in not just His name but who He is as God and what He can do; and then, asked the Lord to help me with my unbelief?
- Can I say in faith it is done... And continue to pray until the mountains move?

HOPELESSNESS

"Be brave. Be strong. Don't give up. Expect God to get here soon."

— PSALM 31:24 THE MESSAGE

It is easy to have hope when things are going well. I usually feel excited and expectant of what I am hoping for will come to term. If I have an anxious thought or fear, I tend to hope for nothing bad to happen. Then, there is hopelessness, and I tend to give up. I feel defeated. There is no use in trying because it is over. It is death to the heart/soul. It is a depression.

Well, I am now 47, and my daughter is 20 years old now. I have been writing these devotions since I was 44 years old. And, yes! We are still battling with addiction and rebellion in my family. Let me tell you, I know what hopelessness feels like. I have had real hope. I have also had negative beliefs that is hoping nothing bad will happen. And I have also reached the pit of hopelessness. I have wallowed in it. It stinks! It is hell on earth!

But, I know feeling hopeless is wrong. Job, David, and many others in the Bible had tastes of hopelessness. They never stayed in that pit of hopelessness. They always remembered who and what their hope was in. It was in God. Christ died on the cross and on the third day rose again to save us and give us hope. From the time of Christ's death until he was resurrected, Christ was in utter hopelessness. The Bible says he ascended into hell. That is utter despair. But, God's power is greater than despair, because Christ was resurrected! Praise God!

In Romans 15:13, it says, "May the God of hope fill you up with joy, fill you up with peace, so you're believing lives, filled with the life-giving energy of the Holy Spirit, will brim over with hope" (The Message Bible). God knows our bodies and souls will experience seasons of hopelessness. Yet, if we are saved, the Holy Spirit, the same power that rose Jesus from the grave, lives in us. The Holy Spirit can fill us with hope again. We must not forget that. I must remember when it seems like nothing will ever change with my daughter. I must be brave, with God's mighty shoulders to support me, and His gentle hands to guide me. I must stand on God's promises. I must expect God to get here soon. I must live in hope and not hopelessness. I must pray that scripture in Romans 15:13 that God will fill me with joy and peace, fill me with life giving energy of the Holy Spirit so my life will brim over with hope.

Dear Lord,

Thank you for sending your Son to die on the cross to give me and all who call upon Him hope. Forgive me for listening to the devil's lies that there is no hope for my child. Help me to be brave and stand on Your Word. Help me expect you to show up in your great timing. I thank you that you are bigger than this addiction. Thank you for my child and the blessings his/her life have given to us even in the bad times. I thank you that your love for my child is greater than I even have for them. I thank you that you will remember my child and answer my prayer because it says in your word that you will. I may be like Abraham and never see my hope fulfilled. But, when I get to heaven I will experience the fullness of hope and see your plan accomplished. I know you have a plan for my life and my child's life. I know you did not strike us with addiction. Like Job, the Devil is trying to pull my child and I away from you. I, like Job, will crawl out of my sense of hopelessness and will declare You as my hope.

Amen

QUESTIONS FOR THOUGHT:

- Through the trials of parenting a child who is bound by addiction, have I given up hope... Am I surrendering to hopelessness... Am I in the pit of depression?
- Do I believe in the Power of the cross? Do I believe in the Power of Jesus?
- Do I know Christ is the source of all hope and my hope is not in this present world, but rests in our future home in Heaven? Do I believe no matter what happens God has a hope and future for my child and me in Heaven?
- Have I received that resurrecting hope fully so no matter what is happening around me I can brim over with hope so others can see Christ in me? And that same hope brimming over in me might touch my child?
- Is my Hope greater than addiction, or am I going to let addiction win?

LISTENING

*"Are you listening to this? Really
listening?"*

— MATTHEW 13:9 THE
MESSAGE

I am not a good listener at all. I get easily distracted
by the things that are going on around me. What I
see and how I feel often deafen my ears to what I
should be listening to. I may hear you, but I usually have
to concentrate really hard to listen well. I find it really
hard to listen to God when I am not seeking Him fully
because His voice is not always audible.

Over the last several years I have been very distracted by
what I see my daughter doing, and I have been very

overwhelmed by emotions/feelings over having a wayward child. I find it hard to listen to normal conversations at work and even around friends and family because I am so in tune to the negative noise in my life. I often have realized that I hear the person talking to me, but have really no clue what that person just said because I was not listening!

When you have a wayward child, not only are everyday conversations difficult to listen to but, listening to God can be impossible. I found myself talking and praying to God. I read the words God spoke to me through the scriptures. But, I found it hard to listen to what was being said.

I do remember when I first began to suspect that my daughter was using drugs. I would be praying for God to not let it be true. I would be frantically looking for evidence in her room and things when she was not around. I would be questioning her and her friends. I can even remember my husband and me following her at night in our car. I thought I was very vigilant in my pursuit to find out answers. When I could find no answers to her rebellious behavior, I could only ask God to tell me what I needed to know. I needed God to hear me and I needed to listen for His answer. Believe it or not, I did audibly hear God one night. I was asleep and suddenly awoke. I sat up straight in bed as if someone had called my name. Then, I heard God tell me, "Your daughter is doing drugs!" I not only heard it, but you can be sure I listened. It was not long after that we found out from our daughter that she had been drug tested at school and was more than likely going to fail it. I was listening for sure at that point.

All of that was at the initial stages of our journey with addiction. Things just got worse afterward. There were numerous battles with our daughter, fights in our marriage, turmoil with our other child, confusion and chaos all around distracted our listening. Those were times it was hard to hear what God was telling us to do. Even in present times, when I get so caught up in my initial feelings and reactions, I cannot hear God. I guess I have my "worry" fingers stuck in my ears so I do not have to listen.

God talks to me through his Word, through other Christians; through music, through dreams, and within my heart and soul. He is not always audible. But, I must clear my heart and mind of all that is not from God: worry, fear, anxiety, lies, deceit, anger, and denial, in order to hear God- really listen to God. If I am a Christian, Christ lives in me. I should be able to hear someone who lives in me, right? Matthew Chapter 13 verse 16 states that we have special ears blessed by God to hear. I am pretty sure that means that I have the Holy Spirit in me now and a direct link to hear/listen to what God is saying. I don't hear Him because of all the clutter noise from emotions and feelings. I don't hear because of the fingers I have stuck in my ears; because it might be hard to deal with what God might have to say.

I have found that I must totally clear my cluttered heart and mind to hear what the Holy Spirit is telling me. I must usually be very still and patient to listen to God. He often whispers and usually waits for me to quite down to really listen to Him. I am still working on my listening, but it is becoming easier because I can recognize the background noise now. I can then start to tune that ugly noise down, and tune into God. I am hopeful that one day my ears will be completely transformed to listening through "God-blessed ears." I can only imagine how listening through those kind of ears will change my relationship with Christ and my relationship with others for the better.

Dear Lord,

Forgive me for being so distracted with the sounds of this world and the words from the Devil. Forgive me for not listening to You first and foremost. Help me settle quickly when those calls from my wayward child come, so that I may listen and hear what You would have me do as a parent.

Amen

ADDITIONAL SCRIPTURE REFERENCES:

"They stick their fingers in their ears so they won't have to listen." Matthew 13:15 The Message

"But you have...And God-blessed ears-ears that hear."
Matthew 13:16 The Message

QUESTIONS FOR THOUGHT:

- Do I find it hard to hear from God?
- Have I only listened to the clutter of the world and to my own feelings and emotions?
- Have I asked God to open my "God Blessed ears" to hear Him and Him only?
- Have I settled, gotten still, focused on what God is telling me, teaching me; reminding me; revealing to me through His Word; through other Believers; through His still, quiet voice? Am I listening...ready to respond... knowing that He knows best, or do I have my fingers stuck in my ears because of my self-absorption with my child addict?

DISAPPOINTMENT

"Though the cherry trees don't blossom
    and the strawberries don't ripen,
    Though the apples are worm-eaten and
    the wheat fields stunted, Though the
    sheep pens are sheepless and the cattle
    barns empty, I'm singing joyful praise
    to God. I'm turning cartwheels of joy
    to my Savior God. Counting on God's
    Rule to prevail, I take heart and gain
    strength. I run like a deer. I feel like
    I'm king of the mountain!"

— HABAKKUK 3: 17-19 THE
MESSAGE

How hard it is to overcome the deep disappointment of my very own flesh and blood rebelling against everything I have taught her? It is so hard to find joy or sing praises during such times and a difficult situation to process. My child's suffering breaks my heart.

I remember when my scary suspicion was confirmed. My daughter was showing all the classic symptoms of using drugs. She was confining herself to her room, losing interest in activities she used to find fun, sleeping a lot, showed declining grades, changing friendships, and having an overall rotten attitude. God woke me up in the middle of the night, and He told me that my daughter was doing drugs. Two days afterward, she came to us and revealed she had been drug tested at school and was more than likely going to fail. My heart dropped. Our world was about to change forever.

My daughter was an honor roll student throughout middle school, the same daughter who always dreamed of being a cheerleader in college. She cheered in middle school and her freshman and sophomore year in high school. She was also on a competitive cheer team. As a parent, I never pressured her about her grades or whether she cheered. These were things she wanted and worked hard at achieving. Her group of friends changed during her freshman year of high school. Her grades dropped with each nine weeks from freshman year through sophomore year. Cheerleading was less important, and she would always try to find an excuse to miss competitive cheer practice. With the now confirmed drug issue, she stopped cheering at the end of her sophomore year and struggled for the rest of her high school year to even make it into a college because of her grades. But, these were minor, insignificant issues compared to our family conquering this now dooming drug problem. Disappointment is almost an understatement! I was devastated, everything I had done to nurture and develop in my daughter was now ravished by drugs. My so called perfect family life seemed destroyed. Our plans for the future and our finances stunted now.

Thank goodness God understands! I found comfort in the verses from Habakkuk 3:17-19. Even though the verses are talking about crops and farm animals, these represent things of value. They are examples of things you spend time nurturing, tending to, loving, and anxiously waiting to bloom, mature and grow. I could see the parallel, my daughter would not blossom or grow the way I had dreamed or the way I had planned. But it was evident my plans and goals were not a part of God's plan. I do not think my daughter choosing to do drugs was God's plan, but it was her choice/decision, and God now had to help us through it. And that is why the second part of the verse is so beautiful! My daughter will speak of wanting to change, and she will temporarily make small changes. When I hear these things, I know deep down she does not want to be an addict. It's then I try to focus on these glimpses of hope that one day she will realize her lifestyle must change. Because of God's word, I can count on Him to prevail, and I have this hope as my strength.

I am thankful now and then, when I see her realizing her life is not what it is meant to be. I keep hoping she will lay her guilt, shame, and addiction down at the foot of the cross. He will win this fight we are struggling with! I am counting on God to restore my daughter and my family. That is the reason I can be joyful and sing praise. I am protected like the deer because I have a place to run when things get rotten and empty; and I am like the king of the mountain because my God is ultimately victorious over the world.

Dear Lord,

I hate being disappointed especially about my child. I can only imagine how You feel when we disappoint You. Please forgive me for all the times I don't measure up; all the times I fail to bloom and when I produce rotten fruit; all the times I let the sheep pens and barns stay empty. I thank You that You rule and I don't. I thank You for being my Provider, my Hope, my Strength. I thank You that You will be victorious in the life of my child who is a Christian, one of Your children. I love you, Lord.

Amen

QUESTIONS FOR THOUGHT:

- Even though my life is not going as planned and things are not as they should be, am I praising God anyway?
- Am I counting on God's rule to prevail?
- Can I cling to that promise and gain strength, be free, and know I am more than a conqueror through Christ? Or am I going to wallow in the loss of the things of this world?

PART III

ANCHORED

So, you have thrown in your anchor, and you have gone deep with God. Now you have given Him your anger and your guilt. With an open heart, you have received forgiveness and have forgiven. Courageously, you have surrendered your fears and substituted His strength for your weakness. You have acknowledged spiritual warfare and are ready to battle as a mighty warrior of God. You have cast all your worry and anxiety unto Him. You have diminished sleeplessness. You expect pain and suffering to come in this world, yet can stand firm and survive with God at your side. You have relinquished apathy and emptiness to the grave and strive to live a full life. You have renewed your faith and cast off hopelessness. You are listening to God and can openly praise His name in spite of disappointment. As you surrendered all the above to God, you now can be anchored to the Rock in the midst of this storm of addiction with your child. You may be swayed by the wind, rain, and waves to come, but your hope is in God alone. By being anchored in Him, you will receive Joy. You will also have thankfulness, you will understand through God's eyes, you will run your race, you will know you are a part of God's plan, and you will know how deep and how wide God's love is for you.

JOY

*"Until now you have not asked anything in
my name. Ask and you will receive,
and your joy will be complete."*

— JOHN 16:24 NIV

I literally write this chapter at a time when I don't feel joy in human terms. I could not be in a more unhappy place speaking in the flesh. My life I have now is not at all what I dreamed it would be. My family is in complete upheaval and if left up to my flesh I would get out now. But, these thoughts are all based on feelings of unhappiness and disappointment; as well as, not getting my way. This is definitely not joy seen as fruit of the Spirit.

Jesus says that He came that all may have joy. I am a Believer, and I must choose joy in the midst of my trials. I may not feel happy at present, but I have joy because Christ lives in me and He is the source of my joy even when I feel so unhappy. As Christians, we are never promised a life free of problems, sorrow, pain or regret. Instead, the Bible even says we should be joyful during these times.

I have prayed and prayed in Jesus name for my rebellious child to turn away from her sin. I have prayed that God immediately heals my family. But, that prayer has not been answered yet. The pain and trouble are still present. God spoke to me through a song on the radio. The song is about someone going through a storm in life. In the main chorus of this song, the words expressed are basically that the person is going through a very painful circumstance and she doesn't know what on Earth God is doing, but the singer exclaims that she still knows who God is.

This is joy in the midst of heartache. I must remember God is who He is today and forever. God is good. God is love. God is healer. God understands. God answers my prayers. God's ways are not my ways. God's timing is His own and not mine. God knows the bigger picture. God saves. God is for me. For all of these reasons, I must choose to be joyful even in bad situations. I must make my requests in Jesus' name and know that my prayers have been heard and rejoice in that alone. I must remember that God is victorious over evil and that even if not on earth my peace and ultimate happiness/joy is waiting for me in Heaven.

My wayward child can make me feel so unhappy. My child, however, is not my source of joy. My joy is from God. When my drug-addicted child leaves me feeling sad, I have to turn my focus to God and ask Him to fill me with joy. Then immediately, thank God for all He has done in the past and for all He will do in the future for me, my child and my family. I choose to thank Him for the little things that evoke feelings of happiness in my day such as a laughing baby; a funny joke; the timely call from a dear friend; the love of others in my family. I chose to reach out and serve others. Nothing brings greater joy than serving others and making others happy. I must keep my focus on God, not my problems with my child. I give these problems to God. I pray every second if I have to, in order to keep the devil from stealing my joy.

Dear Lord,

I feel so unhappy. I hate that I let the choices my child has made make me feel unhappy and leave me joyless. Forgive me for losing focus from You. I thank You that I know who You are even though I don't get or understand what You are doing. In the midst of my trial, I ask that You fill my heart with Your joy! Thank you that You are my source of joy and no one or nothing can be that source of joy for me. -*Amen*

QUESTIONS FOR THOUGHT:

- Am I relying on my situation with my drug addict child to change for me to have joy?
- Do I know the difference between happiness and Joy? Do I know that happiness is a feeling and that Joy is the fullness of God living in and working through me?
- Do I understand that I have to choose Joy? Do I understand that I have to move away/run from darkness and unhappiness or I will fall into its pit?
- Do I seek Joy by looking for Jesus/God in my everyday world?

THANKFULNESS

"We must be careful not to stir up discontent, discontent destroyed them."

— 1 CORINTHIANS 10:10 THE MESSAGE

We are to be thankful, regardless of the circumstances. God's word declares it and I know I am to be content in all situations, but it is not the easiest of tasks. God does not like grumbling. This has stomped my toes many times over the past years. In the midst of experiencing the difficulties of a wayward child and journeying through the devastation of a loved one overcome by drug addiction, God wants me to approach Him with a heart of thankfulness. I know I am supposed to be thankful, but it is difficult. It is not always my initial response but the beginning of God's teaching me to be thankful in all things.

I have hated and still hate what my daughter and my family have experienced over the past several years. I grumbled and complained to God in the midst of praying for relief and deliverance of this horrific situation. I guess you would say I was acting like one of those Israelites wandering in the desert. I was trying to follow God. I hated the situation He seemed to have put me in. I was complaining about how horrible everything was. I was pleading for Him to help me get out of this situation and to turn my daughter back to the way she was before.

Grumbling and complaining put me way down in a dark pit I wanted out of desperately. God showed me how grumbling and complaining only deepened my pain and depression. Through devotions, church sermons, and people, God reminded me of His sovereignty. He taught me to be thankful in all my circumstances. Thank goodness it was God showing me, instead of someone else. Only God would have the patience and forgiveness to teach me this lesson because I kept going back to grumbling and complaining even when He was showing me the way through "this desert" I was traveling. Anyone else would have quit on me-given up on my unteachable spirit.

Initially, through the first episodes of dealing with a

wayward child with drug addiction, I was in such pain and shock I could only cry and have a pity party. I could not muster up an ounce of thankfulness at all, even though I had been reading my Bible, and I knew I should be thankful in all situations. God was so merciful towards me. One day I heard His still small voice say to me, "Just be thankful you are breathing. Just breathe in and out today. Just be grateful I provide you air and a working body to breathe." And, that was the first time I could thank God in the midst of pain and turmoil.

The next thing God showed me was life through His eyes. When you are looking at life through human eyes in the midst of trouble, things are gray, dull, and stagnant. God asked me to look for Him in my world around me. God is not gray, dull, nor stagnant. So, I looked for things He created in this world for me to enjoy: beautiful sunsets; the night sky full of stars; a beautiful flower; a cute puppy; a giggling baby; a deep soulful patient I was working with; chirping birds; soft sweet breezes. I was thankful for the little things God was providing for me during this terrible time- things only He could create. Things that showed me He is in control. Many of these things I could be thankful for when everything was so bleak. Out of becoming thankful, I crept out of a pit to find joy and laughter again; another thing I could be thankful for.

After a while, when I would grumble and fall into an emotional pit again, I would force myself to find something to be thankful for. It might be hearing of a situation worse than mine and being thankful my daughter was still alive. It might be thankfulness for the essentials like food, clothing and a roof over my head. It might be thankfulness for the husband, son, and family I have. It might be thankfulness for the job I have where I can help others and be away from my life for a moment. It might be thankfulness for a kind stranger or thankfulness for the wonderful friends God had given me in recent years. It definitely is being thankful God does control in spite of our desperate situations. Before long, the pain and suffering were being dulled by my being thankful and "God's Joy" was replacing my human sorrow.

Not that I still don't have pity parties and I don't stumble into grumbling again. I do! But I now remove myself from those feelings before I fall into that terrible pit! Negativity is a black hole. Grumbling and complaining are devil's trap of the soul. Being thankful creates a cleansing of a foul heart. It is praising God for who He is, He was, and who He will be! It is a realization that God is in control. He is worthy of all my praises for He is good and His love for me is everlasting no matter what my situation is at the moment. Being thankful keeps me from self-destruction and protects me from the devil's evilness.

God taught me to be thankful even when I did not think it was possible. Sometimes life is so cruel that I cannot find it in myself to be thankful. But God's greatness makes me thankful! I hope after reading this, someone going through a similar situation will just ask God to show them how to be thankful. I know from experience, He will. He hates grumbling and complaining. It does nothing for Him, or for us. Being thankful brings honor and glory to God. We cannot do it enough for what He deserves. He will show us how to be thankful if we seek His help.

Dear Lord,

Thank you for teaching me to be thankful. Right now, I thank you for not punishing me for my negative attitude and grumbling about the way I thought you were handling things. Father, thank you for returning my contentment in the midst of trouble. Most of all, thank you, Lord, for a soft place to land when I fall.

Amen

ADDITIONAL SCRIPTURE REFERENCES:

"Praise the Lord. Give thanks to the Lord, for he is good; his love endures forever. Who can proclaim the mighty acts of the Lord or fully declare his praise?" Psalm 106: 1-2 NIV

QUESTIONS FOR THOUGHT:

- Am I grumbling and complaining like the Israelites in the desert-when God is right there showing me the way and providing for all my physical, emotional and spiritual needs?

- Am I thankful for Jesus dying on the cross and saving me? Is there anything else He has to do? Do I not see how He not only saved me, but He continues to pour down a blessing on me anyway?

- Am I so blinded by my child's addiction, I cannot even see what God is doing and will do for me?

- Can I ask God to show me how to be thankful in the midst of this circumstance? Can I search for God in this chaos? When I find Him, can I thank Him for everything?

UNDERSTANDING

"We don't yet see things clearly. We're squinting in a fog, peering through a mist. But it won't be long before the weather clears and the sun shines bright! We'll see it all then, see it all as clearly as God sees us, knowing him directly just as he knows us!"

— 1 CORINTHIANS 13:12 THE MESSAGE

D o you get it? When we understand, we have a clear visual picture of what is happening, why it is happening, and the reason something is going on. As a Christian parent, I have a real hard time understanding why my daughter became a drug addict. In my mind, I have concluded something must have happened to her in those teen years that caused a deep, painful wound. I don't know what it is or what it was, I only know from listening and reading between the lines of my daughter's communication with me that something happened and she cannot get over it. My guess is she uses drugs to avoid the pain and mental anguish about that life crushing event that occurred. But it is only a guess. I do not have a real understanding of why she uses drugs.

As a Christian, I have had a difficult time understanding why drug addiction has struck our family. If you want me to be honest, I have trouble understanding how to deal with some of the issues that arise with loving a drug addict. It is hard to get a clear picture of what God is doing and what He wants me to do as a parent. It all gets cloudy and confusing at times, especially when you think your child has conquered the addiction only to find out she relapsed into that ugly world again. So far, it has been more than four years that we have been battling this addiction and rebellion in our family. I still don't get it!

I don't get how a beautiful blue-eyed blonde girl, who was born with an adventurous personality bound by a heart of gold, could destroy herself as she does. I don't get how my child who has the world at her fingertips could just blow it all away for a drug rush or escape. I do not understand how my "saved at six years old" daughter, my daughter who led others to Christ as a child could be this far from God now. I do not understand why she keeps running from God when I know God is right there to rescue her if she would just surrender everything to Him.

In my mind, I have guesses, intuition, and gut feelings about who, what, when, and why all these questions exist, but no clear understanding of the whole picture. Frankly, I cannot see clearly enough through the fog of pain, disappointment, anger, and sadness at times to understand what God is doing. No, I haven't figured it out yet.

Thankfully, with God as my guide, I have found I'm not required to understand. For God's ways are not my ways. God is God, and I am me. With my strength, I can only hold on to His Word and His promises to understand there are reasons and a plan behind all this turmoil. In my power, I can only trust all is being worked for good. I can only know God is here walking with me each day. I can only try to understand God's love and seek His wisdom. I can only hope one day I will understand all this chaos, and the chaos will be nothing but a beautiful picture my God created out of ashes!

Dear Lord,

I cry out for a reason for all this, I do not understand, and I cannot get my head around it at times. Please just give me peace that surpasses all understanding each day. Let me experience You in the midst of my fog. Thank you that you understand even when I do not. -*Amen*

QUESTIONS FOR THOUGHT:

- Can I admit I do not understand why my child is bound by drug addiction?
- Will I trust God has the answers why and He has the big picture, and it is complete?
- Can I trust He will bring forth beauty from ashes?
- Will I take the time to understand who I am in God and understand what God is to me in the midst of this turmoil?

RUNNING THE RACE

"Do you see what this means-all these
pioneers who blazed the way, all these
veterans cheering us on? It means we'd
better get on with it. Strip down, start
running and never quit."

— HEBREWS 12:1 THE MESSAGE

I wish I could tell you specifically how to finish this race we are in. The race a parent of a wayward child must run is long and treacherous. There are times of rest and refreshing along the way. But, it is an uphill battle or a slippery downward slope where bumps and bruises are plentiful.

Having a wayward child, a child bent on rebellion, a child

whose body ruled by drugs, a child whose soul is tricked by the demon of addiction, a child whose spirit is far from God, is a challenging race to run. As a parent of this type child, you are running a race against things beyond your own physical and mental strength. But, these things you are running against are not bigger than God. He is greater!

Some say God gives his toughest battles to his strongest warriors. Now, I'm not sure I am a fighter, and I do not feel strong at times. In fact, I feel like a worn, beaten down slave at times. Yet, if I read of the saints before us like David and Daniel, I realize they were just plain people like me. God made them into warriors. They relied on God for strength and perseverance. These saints of old made huge mistakes and suffered in their lives even though they followed God. Yet, they became mighty warriors for God, and through them, God fulfilled His plan. They finished the race before them by faith without ever receiving the prize here on Earth.

As a Christian, I run the race with a piece of the prize, Christ, within me and ahead of me. My victory is because of the finished work of Christ, and I run my race through constant prayer for my child, endless unconditional love for my child, and constant cleansing of my heart and forgiveness of the offenses thrown my way. My race is run through living my life as an example of Christ for my child to see; and through donning my Spiritual weapons (truth; righteousness; peace; faith; and salvation) to finish the race against the devil.

So, yes I am a parent of a wayward child. My child, I never quit praying for, was taken away from us because of drugs. I will not give up hope on my child. I will run the race before me for God is with me, and He wins the race for me. I will not let Satan get the best of my family or me during this trial. Even if the drugs take my daughter's life, I will continue to run the race. I will continue to run straight towards God and take as many with me as I can. I will run the race of helping as many parents with wayward children as I can. My race is to stay close to God in the midst of trouble, to be obedient to His ways, to love and help others as He has helped me. I cannot as a parent race to save my child from drugs that is her race she must run. I can only stay my course, my race, and help others along the way. As a parent, I can only love her, provide wisdom, and be an example of Christ to her.

Dear Lord,

Thank you for this race I love and hate at the same time. I hate the pain and discomfort from the race at times. I love the closeness I have gained with you in this race. I love the fact I am victorious in you. I ask you show me how to be a good parent to my wayward child. I ask you to give me wisdom on steps I need to take to draw him/her closer to you. I ask you protect my child in their race. I ask you get his/her attention so he/she may see you as the leader of his/her race and get off the path he/she is running towards. I love You, Lord. -*Amen*

QUESTIONS FOR THOUGHT:

- Am I in the race with Christ behind me, within me, and before me?
- Do I know my part in this race even though I cannot control the other racers and the outcome?
- Do I realize the race is already won and all the saints in heaven are cheering me on to finish my part in the race? Do I realize those saints know how great the finish line is and are roaring in Heaven for me not to quit no matter the difficulties and roadblocks?

GOD'S PLAN

"For I know the plans I have for you,"
declares the Lord, "plans to prosper
you and not to harm you, plans to give
you hope and a future."

— JEREMIAH 29:11 NIV

This verse has been our family verse during these long, battling years with our daughter. We had this verse printed on her Senior ad for her high school yearbook. My husband has this verse tattooed on his shoulder. We recall this verse in our times of struggle and doubt.

It has been several years since she went to her first rehab at Teen Challenge in Arizona. She has been in multiple rehabs since, and she has seen several psychiatrists and medical doctors all to help her with her addiction. It is and has been a never-ending journey with brief glimpses of hope the battle is done, and addiction of drugs has been replaced with an addiction to God.

Our daughter made it a month of being "clean," close to finding a job, looking for volunteer work, and going to church with us for four Sundays in a row. I thought, "This is it! She's got it," only to be punched in the gut; she started doing drugs again. Same song and dance: being unusually sick; sleeping the days away; defiant attitude; nonchalant behavior; hanging with the old buds; not leaving bad relationships when the opportunity arose.

My husband, son, and I were thoroughly frustrated and exhausted. Once again, we had to enforce another horrible intervention, to demonstrate her choices would not affect our principles nor our lives. We had to tell her she could not be with us while under the influence of drugs. So, time has passed with no communication and no seeing our daughter. Such a grievance time, so difficult, so painful; yet, a strange peace of knowing God has this too. I love The Message Bible's version of Jeremiah 29:11: "I know what I'm doing. I have it all planned out-plans to take care of you, not abandon you, plans to give you the future you hope for". Sometimes, it makes little sense in my mind, how God works. But, the Holy Spirit reassures me He has this and will turn it all around.

There are verses in the Bible that declare this promise. Romans 8:28 states, "God works for the good of those who love Him, who have been called according to His purpose." Psalm 46:10 says, "Be still and know I am God." A new favorite verse I am claiming is from Micah 7:7. It states, "But me, I'm not giving up. I'm sticking around to see what God will do. I'm waiting for God to make things right. I'm counting on God to listen to me".

So, I will continue to be obedient in my pain, and in my moments of doubt, I will seek His face. I will claim Jeremiah 29:11 and follow it with Micah 7:7.

Dear Lord,

I know you have plans for me, to not harm me, and to give me the future I hope for. Amen. Amen. I am not giving up. I am sticking it through to the end to watch for your beautiful redeeming plan to unfold. I know you hear my cry.

Amen

QUESTIONS FOR THOUGHT:

- Do I know God has a plan for my life and for my child's life?
- Am I willing to follow God and take His lead for my life or am I going to go my way? Am I ready

to believe this life my family is living, and my child is living, was never intended by God? -He wanted none of this...so am I going to follow God or am I going to allow the devil to take me down to the pit?

GOD'S KNOWLEDGE

*"You know when I leave and when I get
back, I am never out of your sight"*

— PSALM 139:3 THE MESSAGE

God knows everything about me. He knew me before I was in my mother's womb. He knows the number of hairs on my head. He knows my name. He knows my thoughts and my heart. He knows the universe and all of its makings because He is Creator of it all.

God knows the plan he has for me. He knows my good days and my bad days ahead. He is for me and not against me. He does not come to make my life miserable and heap trouble on me to see if I can muddle through it. He wants me to have a good future and hope as I get there.

Ultimately, our future is in heaven. But I believe God wants me to have a future here on Earth, even though it is temporary. I live in a fallen world prowled by Satan. Satan does not want me to have hope, nor a future. Satan plans evil and wants to destroy me. So, life here on Earth will never be perfect. My future will not be perfect until I am in Heaven. I will have trouble here on Earth. God knows this and even tells me this in his Word.

God knows my daughter, and God knows me. He did not create my child to be an addict nor me to suffer as a parent of an addict. My child made a bad choice one day for whatever reason. My child had something happen to her or within her that the devil used to pull her into his ways and pull her away from God ways. None of this was a part of God's original plan. God knows the plans he has for my daughter. He is waiting for his "prodigal" daughter to come to her senses and return "home."

God knows every terrible choice my daughter made. He knows every terrible act I made as a parent. In this knowledge, God still sent His son, Jesus to save my daughter and me. He offers me the gift of grace. He will not force it upon me. One does not force a gift onto anyone. You can only receive a gift if you accept. Once we turn back to God, then He steps in to deliver us to a future and fill us with hope.

God knows how this whole ordeal will turn out. He knows the next steps in His plan. It would be easy for God to just fix it immediately. I believe He has the power to do so, but He is waiting because He knows best. It is written He knows how to turn what was meant for evil into good for those who love Him. I will hold to God's knowledge being greater than what I know to sustain me through this crisis.

Dear Lord,

Thank you that you know! Thank you that you know my thoughts and my heart. Thank you that you love me anyway. Thank you that you know the plans you have for me, and nothing will deter those ultimate plans. Thank you that the mistakes I make may lead me off the expected path temporarily, but you ultimately know the way if I follow. Thank you that you know and love my child. Thank you that you have his/her in your sight and thoughts. Thank you that your ways are greater. Thank you that You know how this is all going to end.

Amen

ADDITIONAL SCRIPTURE REFERENCES:

"Your thoughts-how rare, how beautiful! God, I'll never comprehend them." Psalm 139:17 NIV

QUESTIONS FOR THOUGHT:

- Do I realize how much God loves me? Do I accept He knows me inside and out and still loves me?
- Do I understand I live in a fallen world, and what happened to my child with drugs is not God's will? Do I know God is for me and not against me?
- Can I accept and claim the Gift of Jesus Christ as my Savior, my redeemer? Can I rest in the fact all those who believe in Him will be resurrected and forever be free of the chains this world places on us?
- Can I agree God knows best; His plan is best; I should follow Him all the days of my life no matter how this storm of addiction ends? Can I agree it is up to me to accept God's gift of grace or I can choose to stay in my chains?

AFTERWORD

I truly hope these devotions rescue you in the way they rescued me during this terrible trial in life. God truly blessed me in the midst of a crazy, mean storm. I found I could be calm, still, and anchored in His presence with a raging, stormy ocean of drug addiction surrounding me. At the time I began writing this devotional book, I hoped my daughter would come to her senses and be transformed and on fire for God, changing other's lives for the better. I never stopped believing God would answer my prayer in His timing, but I had to get my focus on my Lord. I had some harsh lessons about trust, doubt and God's sovereignty to learn as God held on to me and as I held on to Him in this storm. I had to become anchored in Him.

I need you to know God answered my prayer, but He

answered it in a way He knew best. My sweet Ashlynn was not healed here on Earth. Instead, she was healed on the other side of Glory-in Heaven-in the welcoming arms of her Lord and Savior, Jesus Christ. Ashlynn went to lead a drug-free life, healed in the presence of God on January 30, 2016.

I believe Ashlynn had great potential to live a life bringing others to the Lord. She was an amazing child who led many of her friends to Christ. She was a determined, strong-willed child that would have been a mighty warrior for God. The devil did not like this. She had some trials in her life growing up that wounded her deeply. The devil had stepped in and began lying to her and confusing her thoughts. She experienced deep pain and sorrow and turned to drugs to numb her emotions-yet another scheme of the devil. The devil placed a stronghold on her that was overwhelming for a chemically altered brain. She would have difficulty reasoning and rationalizing to overcome her addiction.

God showed up so many times during these five years to rescue her; she just could not hear it or see it because she was allowing the devil to speak louder to her than she was allowing God. She understood God's capacity to forgive, and she could forgive others so easily. She could not forgive herself, and this is where the devil kept her in chains. So many of us as Christians are trapped like that. We are free, but we choose to remain in the chains. We choose to believe the lies of the devil.

Ashlynn, I truly believe had a true "addictive" brain. It took one time of doing drugs to fuel the fire. Once she took heroin, she was hooked, and her mind became so chemically altered she couldn't see any other way to survive life but to continue to use drugs. The devil thought he had won. He stole her joy and freedom she had in Christ, and he almost took my family and my freedom in Christ. But God showed me the battle was already won. He would heal her if not on Earth then in Heaven because she was a child of God. I think God knew He could best rescue her and save others through her death. God's ways are not our ways. His thoughts are higher than our thoughts. God is God, and I am not!

While her death is excruciating, I can indeed say it is not as painful as watching her live in the captivity of drugs. Drugs are a demon, and they reap hell on everyone. It was awful seeing her in pain and trapped in Hell on Earth. I think if Ashlynn could mentally submit all to God she might have been healed here on Earth. I know God knew there was no other way for her to be healed but in Heaven. I believe through her death many lives will be changed and Jesus will be glorified. I believe if her life had been taken earlier, I would not be the person I am today. God took a terrible storm of drug addiction to anchor me in Him so when He healed her in Heaven, I would be grounded and secure in this new trial of life here on Earth-life with my daughter in Heaven.

While I miss her terribly and I get a "homesick" feeling

when I think of her, I know where she is now and I know she is free, happy, and at peace. She is smiling and full of joy. She is the person God always intended her to be now. That's what happens when we get to Heaven- we are complete in Him and we are finally Home!

My prayer is for you to be anchored in God as you press on to the prize at the end of your storm. "We have Hope as an anchor for the Soul" (Hebrews 6:19). I pray for protection and healing over you and your children. I pray for abundant peace as you submit yourselves and your child completely to the Lord. I pray for lives to be saved unto Him for God ultimately wins, and God does Heal!

ABOUT THE AUTHOR

DEBORAH BAILEY is the co-founder of the Ashlynn Bailey Foundation, and with her husband, Mike, they are committed to raising awareness and ministering to parents of addicts. Deborah and Mike reside in the Birmingham, Alabama area with their son.

For More Information:
ashlynnbaileyfoundation.com

CPSIA information can be obtained
at www.ICGtesting.com
Printed in the USA
BVHW01s2033281117
501447BV00009B/202/P